# LEARNING SOCIAL MICRO AND MACRO ECONOMIC BEHAVIORAL CHANGES



JOHN LOK

# Contents

# Preface

Introduction

What are the different unique characteristics between one developing country and one developed country ? How to judge whether the country had been either developed or had been developing ? What factors influence the country development speed? In my this book, I shall indicate New Zealand whether is one developed country or developing country, although its farming industry , e.g. sheep cloth manufacturing, breef and pork meat food export industries had developed long time, but what weaknesses, it owns to influence its continue development easily as well as what strengths it lacks to influence New Zealand is still staying in the developing stage in possible in global leading position. What factors influence US, UK their technological development can not be continued innovated to cause worse development to compare Germany 's heavy manufacturing industry future development in possible.

In our societies, how developing and developed countries can apply robotics to improve themselves countries social development to be better, even the best. Can robotic development be applied to help developed and developing noth to improve their societies in success? Can robotic development only be applied to help developed countries to improve their societies more easier to compare developing countries? Is it difficult or it is not possible to apply robotic development to any developing countries?

Behavioral economy is one useful and fun social subject. Behavioral economists ususally research how and why human behaviors may influence economy growth or recession, or how and why economy environment changing factor may influence human behavior changes.

Any organizations must need resources to be provided in order to suppky for their organizational development. However, resouces may include human resources, equipment facilities resources , earth natural resource e.g. land, water wood, gas et. building material resources, even working time resources , technological etc. different kinds of resources. Thus, it seems that any organizations must need some resources to help their organizational daily operation in success.The question concerns what the best resources used strategies to be achieve the most efficiency or the best performance to be organizational development.

How can business apply right or reasonable science management principle to manage that businesses effectively and efficiently in order to achieve sale and profit raising aim in the least resource suitation? Otherwise, applying wrong or unreasonable science management principle , it can bring what disadvantages or negative impacts to the businesses. IN my this chapter, I shall attempt to indicate above questions . Readers can have more clear view whether why the kinds of science resource management methods are not suitable to be applied to the kind of organizations to bring negative impact consequences.

# Prologue

Table Of Content

Methods developing countries can
become developed countries

- Main industries aspects need to develop p.71-80
- The challenges are needed to solve in development process
- What a developing country should do to be a developed one?
- Developed Countries need to help Developing Countries to increase their competitive effort in societies

Can bring global benefit when all
countries are developed countries

1. How Globalization Affects Developed Countries

Conflicting Globalization Views

- Benefits of globalization
- Drawbacks of globalization
- What Is Globalization?
- Why and how globalization may achieve when global countries can develop to become developed countries ?
- Components of Globalization
- The degree to which an organization is globalized and diversified has bearing on the strategies that it uses to pursue greater development and investment opportunities.
- Effect of globalization on developing countries or third world countries
- What influences to the countries like china and India has grown tremendously after globalization.
- Effect of globalization on developed countries when all developing countries can become developed countries
- Development of "Regional economic" will truly help India to build viable economic future for its citizens.
- Regional economies help to reduce domination of developed economies on the developing economies.

2. Economic growth advantages and disadvantages

- Are economic growth and development worthwhile?
- Economic growth and development of Asia when all or many

CHAPTER ONE

# DEFINING DEVELOPED AND DEVELOPING COUNTRIES DIFFERENCES

● What are the developed countries and developing countries characteristics

What factors cause the differences between developed countries and developing countries? Do they have significant unique characteristics to be discovered to influence their differences? I shall attempt to indicate evidences to explain whether these are significant different unique characteristics between any developed countries and developed countries as below:

ON economic measurement aspect, low-and middle income economies are usually referred to as developing economies , and the upper middle income and the high income are referred to as developed countries. So, a developing country also called a less developed country or emerging market, it has a lower gross domestic product( GDP) than developed countries, with a less nature and sophisticated economy. The difference is between developed and developing countries. It may indicate that developed countries refer to the Sovereign ( independent) nation/state whose economy has highly progressed and possesses great technological improvement, as compared to other nations.

The countries with low industrialization and low human development indix are formed as developing countries. The World Bank classified the world's economies into four groups, based on Gross National Income per capita: high, upper middle, lower-middle , and low income countries. Least developed countries, landlocked developing countries and small island developing states are all sub-groupings of developing countries. However, it is not ensure that it is only all islands are developing countries, e.g. New Zealand may be one developing country or low developed country also. Experts have said the Guyana has one of the fastest -growing economies in the world.

The unique characteristics differences between developed countries and developing countries. They may include: developing countries are ususally poor, according to the Asian development bank, the major causes of poverty may include: Low economic growth, a week agricultural sector, increased population rates and a high volume of inequality. So, the features of developing countries, their common characteristics may include: low per capita real income, low per capita real income is one of the most defining because amony any developed countries , they may also include highly and lowly developed countries. For example, Norway is the most developed nation in the world. Switzerland is the second developed country in the world, Ireland is the third-most developed country. Then all of these nations may be highly developed countries , e.g. Germany, Hong Kong, China, Australia, Iceland, Sweden. So , it seems that New Zealand may be a lowly developed country to compare above these highly developed countries.

- What factors assist the developing countries to become developed countries

However, the most developing countries in the world, they may include India, Brazil, China, Argentina is actually considered a developing country and characteristics of developing economies, high population is continue growing. Otherwise, China had began to use methods to discourage Chinese families to born more than one child in order to avoid population continue grows to bring social future burden.

Dependence on primary sector, e.g. Africa and India and New Zealand , they were still depending on main agricutural fruit, rice primary farming industry for themselves main GDP export income source as well as dependence on exports of primary commodities. So, developing countries should need focus on human development, it will remain the main focus of developing countriespost 2015 year. In this regard, the transition of developed countries to equitable and sustainable consumption will make in easier for developinf countries to pursue their human development goals in a more environmental susttainable way.

Hence, human development will may to help developing countries to develop more easily. It is future essential element to assist any one developing countries to be developed countries in success.

The unique characteristics of developing countries include that: Literacy rate is quite low as people are deprived of education facilities, the standard of living in developing countries is normally not very high. Otherwise, developed countries literacy rate is quite high , due to better education ayatem and life expectancy rate is more , due to better standing living. So, in general, the standard of living is very high to developed countries, e.g. UK, US , they have many the low income level or poor people still may have enough money to save in bank and the number of poor people is less in themselves countries, due to definitional discrepancies countries, such as Maxico, Greece and Turkey. India may be nowadays developing countries.

However, there are agrument or disagreement between developed and developing countries. The developed countries say that developing countries must stop burning fossil, fuels and other things that harm the atmosphere. Otherwise, developing countries argue that developed countries have developed by burning the fossil fuels. They say their development will be affected if they stop burning fuels. For Japan example, it is one highly developed country because ir is one of the largest and most developed economies in the world. It has a well-educated, industrious workforce and its large , affluent population makes it is one of the world's biggest consumer markets. Otherwisem New Zealand is not high technological and industrious developed country, it still depends on agricultural fruits, meats export farming industry for main GDP growth source. So, comparison New Zealand and Japan development speed, New Zealand is one lowly developed country. Otherwise, Japan is one highly developed country in nowadays our society. But, the comparison between New Zealand and China, China is still a developing country , but New Zealand may be one lowly developed country to compare China because Chinese government has repeatedly stated that China is the world's largest developing country, despite rapid economic growth over the past four decades. However, according to the 2018 survey, the United States is the world's most powerful country, following countries may include: Japan, Israel, South Korea, Saudi, Arabia, but the safest country may be Iceland because its crime rate is the least. Although, US, UK may be highly developed countries, but their crime rate may be high position. So, one highly developed country does not represent that it must have the most safest social living environment to let its citizen to feel safe to live. It may be any one highly developed countries themselves failure points.

However, environmental factors may also stop a country from developing because some places experience environmental issues, which can present them from developing, examples might be extremee flooding or desertification social factors may also stop a country from developing, e.g. high crime rate, high unemployed rate, low safe living feeling rate, low living standard, they are some parts of the world have issues that are caused by people to influence any countries continue to develop to be one developed country easily. So, all of these factors can assist any one developing country to become developed country.

CHAPTER TWO

# WHAT FACTORS CAUSE DEVELOPED COUNTRIES CONTINUE DEVELOPED

What factors cause New Zealand to be developed country in success

What factors influence New Zealand is still one lowly developed country? Can New Zealand fight itself country weaknesses to become one highly developed country? I shall attempt to indicate several evidences to explain what factors influence New Zealand can not develop to reach mature social development stage in itself nowadays society are below:

New Zealand is a small population country. It has only 4.8 million . However, there are many NZ people feel poverty to live. The causes of poverty in New Zealand. They may include: income inequality, lack of a simple fund support from government, lack of economic infrastructure, poor access to education, poor access to healthcase, opinion was evenly diviced on the primary cause of child poverty in NZ. Forty percent of NZ people said it was due to economic factors including unemployment, low wages, and rising living costs, the ever-increasing monthly power bills the the NZ government won't regulate or gone down.

However, in NZ, poverty is seen as relative, whereby those suffering deprivation are often struggling to feed their children, living in insecurce circumstances and unable to enjoy a satisfying social life easily to many New Zealanders. As a result, many NZ family members' health suffers and children fail to achieve a sound level of education. IN fact, there is poverty in the midst of prosperity in NZ. There is poverty amidst prosperity: There are around 682,500 people in poverty in this country or one in seven households, including around 220, 000 children .

In general, there are the causes of poverty reasons to any countries, they may include: lack of good jobs / job growth, lack of good education, the second root causes of poverty is a lack of education, a lack of social welfare, weather/ climate change, social injustice, lack of food and water, lack of government support. Although NZ may be belonged to one developed country. But, it is still staying on the lowly developed stage in long time development process. The main factors cause NZ is still one lowly developed country. They may include : lack of good jobs growth in order to let graduates can find good jobs to do and education level can not be improved . What factors cause NZ lacks good job growht and poor education improvement in long time?

In fact, NZ likes many developed countries, its witnessing a transformation in itself economy and employment opportunities. Its traditional exporting sectors , such as dairy, meat, forestry and tourism, remain important drivers of growth. So, NZ's main source of income, they are agricutlural products export, principally meat, dairy products, and fruits and vegetables , crude oil and wood and paper products are also significant. However, the impacts of poverty in NZ, because children in poor communities are three times more likely than the average child to be sick twice as likely to end up in hospital, and sudden unexpected death in infancy rates are more than 6 times higher for infants in the most disadvantaged areas of NZ. These harmful effects run into adulthood in NZ.

What are the most common jobs in NZ? The most popular carre was police officer. SO, when many NZ people hope to seek policeforce jobs. NZ will bring poor job growth development chance to let graduates have plans to develop other professional career in society. Many NZ graduates only consider policeforce jobs, it is one poor social job culture in NZ. However, NZ education is better than America in possible. NZ is definitely superior to the US, in the OECD nations indication, NZ is ranked 3 rd for education quality behinf Finland and Canada, the US ranks about 12 th . Why does NZ still be one lowly developed country in possible, when it can have superior education system?

In fact, NZ ranks highly on most indicators of well-being, but average social level of incomes are low , in general, inequality income were allocated and made NZ economy less developed in the face of shocks, due to low labour productivity factor, low labour productiviey is only partly explained by the farming main industry of the NZ economy and is primarily a consequence of low mulit-factor productivity growth within NZ other industries development, instead of farming industry as well as weak investment on other industries, e.g. technololgical, computer manufacturing , medicine life science drug manufacturing, construction, engineering, e.g. robotic manufacturing etc. different industries development. So, NZ neglects to consider how to develop other industries instead of concentrating on only development on agricultural industry.

However, economic geography is an important factor in NZ's poor productivity performance as the small size and remoteness of the economy diminish its access to global markets, the scale and efficiency of domestic businesses, the level of competition, and the ability to benefit from innovation at the global frontier. All of these many be the main cause weaknesses to NZ countinue development in success.

Moreover, NZ government lacks good policy to support its productivity growth, e.g. lacking to promoting international

connections, none removing barriers to fixed capital investment to NZ domestic any industries development, instead of agricultural industry, accessing benefits of agricultural industry, accessingg benefits by improving urban planninf, enhancing competition and increasing investment in innovation and intangibles.
Hence, poor productivity technological improvement may be on main factor to cause NZ productivity growth is poor. It is main reason to cause NZ is one lowly developed country in long time, because global highly developed countries concerned high technological productivity is expected to be the main driver of income source , in particular via investment in technology and knowledge-based capital. So, any highly developed countries began to believe that economic growth from productivity improvements contributes to welfare through increasing the worker individual income that can be earned from each hour worked, providing individuals with the option to work lesss or consume moew job and service. Hence , NZ lacks high technological productivity improved to let any one talent NZ person can have chance to use his / her talent knowledge to do high technological jobs in order to attribute NZ society and to earn high hour income. NZ is only developing agricultural industry nowadays. SO, agricultural jobs wil be common jobs in NZ developed country. Hence, low technolgical productive improvement may be main factor to influence NZ to be one lowly developed country in long time.

What factors influence US and UK continue development
Why do US and US be a developed country? It has a high-income economy and a very high human development index rating. Ranking 13 th in the world. Today, the UK , US remains one of the world's great powers with considerable economc, cultural , military, scientific, technological and political influence internationally. Why are UK and US econome so strong? It's quality of life is generally considered high, and the economy is quite diversified . The sectors that contibute must be the US, UK 's GDP are services, manufacturing, construction and tourism . Moreover, UK and US

are the world's largest economy by normimal GDP and net wealth and they are the second largest by purchasing power. Themselves nations's economy is fueled by natural resources, a well-developed and high productivity.

It seems that UK and US have a mixed economic development, developed through free market and global economy , which are regulated by their governments to prevent market failure easily.

CHAPTER THREE

# WHAT FACTORS INFLUENCE SOCIAL DEVELOPMENT SPEED

What factors cause why some countries can develop rapidly ? What factors cause some countries develop slowly? It would be hard to find a more fundamental conept for the social development and human development. The social development science is about human societies how we develop, so we had better have some idea to explain how and why what factors cause some countries can develop rapidly , e.g. US, UK, or what factors cause some countries can develop slowly, e.g. China, India. The reaons that there has been a question about the development speed to any countries , it has been an active and influential movement to insist that this was a human social development question. Why does Inida has many years history, otherwise, US has less many years histroy, what factors influence US can develop more rapidly to compare Inida? Even, India seems to be one developing country in nowadays society.

From sociobiology to social development psychology

What factors to India is facing to influence it can not succeed to develop to be highly developed country easily? Human cognitive mechanisms evolved in the Pleistocene, the period from about 2 million years ago, about 10,000 years ago, the end of the last Ice age, MOtivating this choice is the thought that substantial periods of development time are required for significant evoluntionary change, such as social need change, family need change, country need change. Much of Evolutinnary psychology has consisted of reflection on the different countries changing conditions that might have obtained during this perios, and the human development behaviors what would have been most favoured by natural selection given those conditions.

First of all to what influences human feels we need to develop, a lot of human behavior has roots that are far more ancient. Sociability , for instance, is not a uniquely human attribute. But significant changes in the nature of human sociality are evident over historical periods of tens or hundrends of years, presumably because they are due to cultural improvement, or raising human cultural quality , so our cultural improvement psychology influences why some countries can not develop rapidly, such as India does not consider itself Indian cultural level needs to raise significantly. Otherwise, US condiers itself American cultural level need to raise significantly. So, this cultural development reason may explain why India is still one developing country, although, its has many years history to compare US.

Social Development Psychology

Another important point about social development issus, it is the environmental factor, it is one picture to influence why some countries develop rapidly , but some countries still develop slowly. I don nor need to pursue that argument , since the focus will remain on the human development case, and no one could suppose that the social enviroment that human create for, among the other things, the production of new human social behaviors, is simply a consequence of genetically determined human behavior. For example, American hopes that it can create many talent people to help itself country to develop, so talent people development

environment need can influence US can have many talent people to create to help itself country to develop to be highly developed country in short time, e..g. space science, life science etc.
I wished to emphasize particularly the ability of cultural evolution to transform the social development history to different countries issus. It seems clear that humans have learned in quite recent time to construct a remarkably social changing environment for the development for their young. So, any countries their future development, they must depend on how many talent young people, they can create. It is very important issue to influence any one country to develop to be one high developed or low developed or developing country. For that reason their introduction should be seen as representing major cultural improvemernt and social environment factors to influence any countries their future development speed. For this simple example, many further illustrate the point, they indicate that the mobile phone did not exist when I was a child. In fact, it is for hardly more than a decade that it has been for everyday life in developed countries. Ans whereas it may seem only more or less need for people of my generation, for those aged, say 10 to 20 , age, it is as unthinkable to deprived of one's phone as to wander the streets stark naked. Most teenagers move through the would, when this smart phone technological development, it can influence any one feels that it is essential product to our daily need. It is one cultural improvement factor example , it can explain why global many people feel smart phones are essential product to satisfy us need. It is not, therefore, merely behavior that has changed for those who have grown up with the mobile phone, but the social environment can bring indirect to influence any one , even old age feels smart phone need, when old age people can contact many young people , they must own least one smart phone for personal use. So, cultural improvement and social environment changing need both factors can influence any one country may make development decision in short time or long time, when the country people feel that they have urgent social and cultural improvement changing need rapidly.

What are the differences between developing and developed countries

I shall explain the difference between developed and developing countries characteristics as below:

Countries are divided into two major categories by the United Nations, which are developed countries and developing countries. The classification of countries is based on the economic status such as GDP, GNP, per capita income, industrialization, the standard of living, etc. Developed Countries refers to the soverign state, whose economy has highly progressed and possesses great technological infrastructure, as compared to other nations. The countries with low industrialization and low human development index are termed as developing countries. Developed Countries provides free, healthy and secured atmosphere to live whereas developing countries, lacks these things.

The characteristics between developing and developed countries may include as below:

Developed countries means that a country having an effective rate of industrialization and individual income is known as Developed Country. Otherwise, developing Country is a country which has a slow rate of industrialization and low per capita income. Developed countries have low unemployment and poverty, developing countries have usually high unemployment and poverty. developed countries have low infant mortality rate, death rate and birth rate is low while the life expectancy rate is high. Otherwise, developing countries have high infant mortality rate, death rate and birth rate, along with low life expectancy rate. Developed countries have better living conditions and high standard of living, but developing countries have bad living conditions and low standard of living. Developing countries have high GDP from industrial sector income source, otherwise, developed countries have high GDP income from service sector income source. Developing countries have high industrial growth. Otherwise, developed countries, they rely on the developed countries for their growth. Developed countries have high equal of distribution of income, otherwise, developing countries have high unequal of distribution of income. Finally, developed countries have effectively utilized to factors of production, otherwise, developing countries have ineffectively utilized to factors of production. Overall , any thing of developed countries are better than developing countries in nowadays societies.

Between developed and developing countries, one can identify a variety of differences. This differentiation of countries, as developed and developing, is used to classify countries according to their economic status based on per capita income, industrialization, literacy rate, living standards, etc.

● What are Developed Countries?

They have usually these similar characteristics as below:

(1) Developed countries have industrial growth and enjoy flourishing economy. Developed countries experience marked development and growth in the areas such as transportation, business, and education. Developed countries are characterized by a low death rate and low birth rate as well. There is usually a very small gap between the two rates in developed countries.

(2) Developed countries are not characterized by shortcomings. They are well-developed in all fronts and are served well by water supplies, amenities, educational institutions, health care concerns. This is because of the fact that people are endowed with awareness about every possible aspect relating to human existence. The absence of shortcomings in the developed countries is possibly due to the fact there is a low birth rate in these countries. Nutrition is available in plenty to mothers and infants in developed countries.

● What are Developing Countries?

They have usually these similar characteristics as below:

(1) Developing countries depend on the developed countries for help to establish their industries. They have only begun to taste the growth of the economy. Developing countries are in the beginning stages of development in the areas of education, business, and transportation.

(2) Developing countries are characterized by many shortcomings.

These shortcomings include less awareness regarding matters relating to health, poor amenities, shortage in water supply, shortcoming in the area of medical supply, a higher rate of birth rate. The most important and worrying factor in the developing countries is the factor of poor nutrition. Poor nutrition to both mothers and infants is the main concern in the developing countries. Due to high birth rates, the probability of natural diseases is more in developing countries. Hence, the death rates are also eventually high in developing countries. However, since natural diseases increase by high rates in the developing countries, they will have a short population doubling time. In the case of developing countries, there is usually a big gap between the birth rate and the death rate. Infant mortality factor is influenced by the development factor of countries. A developing country for that matter would have higher infant mortality than a developed country.

Overall, economists will differ their different characteristcs from these several aspects as below:

Developed countries display a high level of development. Developing countries: Developing countries display a lower development in different areas such as industrialization, human capital, etc. Developed countries have industrial growth. Developing countries depend on the developed countries for help to establish their industries. Developed countries enjoy flourishing economy. Developing countries begin to taste the growth of the economy. Developed countries experience marked development and growth in the areas such as transportation, business, and education. Developing countries are in the beginning stages of development in the areas of education, business, and transportation. Developed countries are characterized by a low death rate and low birth rate as well. There is usually a very small gap between the two rates in developed countries. In developing countries there is usually a big gap between the birth rate and the death rate. Hence, in overall, any aspects are worse, slow growth to developing countries compare to developed countries.

● What are general their GDP difference

Developed Countries:

A developed nation is one that has a very high rank in industrial advancement, constructs its economy in light of innovation and assembling rather than agribusiness. The variables of production, for example, human and regular assets are completely used bringing about an increment underway and utilization which prompts a very high rank in per capita salary. A nation with a more Human Development Index (HDI) is viewed as a developed nation. It not just measures the financial improvement and GDP of a nation additionally its instruction and future.

Developing Countries:

A developing nation is those having a way of life or level of modern advancements well beneath that conceivable with money related or specialized guide; a nation that is not yet exceptionally industrialized. A country having less utilization of resources and low income per capita which leads to low GDP of a country.

● Developed VS Developing Countries will have different development or growth speed to compare as below:

?Industrial Economies:

In developed countries, economy depends on industrial sector instead of agriculture sector. There is more development in industrial sector. In developing countries, mostly economy depends on agriculture sector and they are moving toward industrialization.

?Citizens:

In developed countries, citizens and well off and rich. In developing countries, proportion of rich citizens is very low.

?Unemployment:

In developed countries, there is no such issue of unemployment. They provide many employment opportunities to the citizens. In developing countries, issue of unemployment is there and it affects the economy of country very badly.

?Education:

The growth rate in education sector is very high in developed countries and they have best education systems. Whereas the growth rate of developing countries in education sector is low as compare to developed countries. While developing countries are following the education system of developed countries to achieve the standard.

?Technological advantages:

In developed countries, every place is full with technological advancements and they always try to make it better. In developing countries, there are many undeveloped rural areas and even urban sector have less technological advancements.

?Roads:

Developed countries have a very sound infrastructure by having better roads, railway tracks, airports etc. Developing countries don't have a sound infrastructure as compare to developed countries.

?Government:

There exists stable government in developed countries so that they make effective and reliable policies for better economic development. Developing countries have unstable governments and mostly try to following the policies made by developed countries.

?Health care:

In developed countries, good and better facilities for health have been provided to citizens. In developing countries, health care facilities are not so good and acceptable.

?Resources:

In developed countries, the natural and human resources are fully and efficiently consumed. In developing countries, many of the natural resources are still untouched and others resources are also not fully utilized.

?Income:

There is a high level of income as per citizen living in developed country so that they have high GDP and GNP. Developing countries have low level of income as per citizen living in country with unequal distribution of income as that have low GDP and GNP.

?High Human Development Index (HDI):

In developed countries, there are best education systems and better health care and high income level so this leads to high value and ranking of HDI. In developing countries, there are low income level and fewer facilities for health care and low rates of education so this leads to low or middle ranking in HDI.

?Life expectancy:

In developed countries, due to better health care the life expectancy has been increased and they have low birth rates as well as low death rates. In developing countries, life expectancy is not so high but has high rates of birth and death due to less facilities and education.

?Water and food supply:

In developed countries, safe and clean water is supplied with plentiful supply of food items and good housing condition. In developing countries, dirty and unsafe water is supplied with less reliable food items and poor condition of houses.

In conclusion, all our daily necessary need and social need to developing countries growth will be worse to compare developed countries in our nowadays societies.

● How to measure the difference between developed and developing countries ?

The measurement factors between developed and developing countries may include as below:

(1) GDP factor

The classification of a country does not only depend on its income but also on other factors that affect how their citizens live, how their economies are integrated into the global system, and the expansion and diversification of their export industries. A developed country is one that has a high level of industrial development, bases its economy on technology and manufacturing instead of agriculture. The factors of production such as human and natural resources are fully utilized resulting in an increase in production and consumption which leads to a high level of per capita income. A country with a high Human Development Index (HDI) rating is considered a developed country. It not only measures the economic development and GDP of a country but also its education and life expectancy. A developed country's citizens enjoy a free and healthy existence.

(2) Industralization or Commercial aspect factor

The term "developed country" is synonymous to "industrialized country, post-industrial country, more developed country, advanced country, and first-world country." The United Kingdom, France, Germany, Canada, Japan, Switzerland, and the United States of America are only a few of those considered as developed countries. A developing country, on the other hand, is one that has a low level of industrialization.

It has a higher level of birth and death rates than developed countries. Its infant mortality rate is also high due to poor nutrition, shortage of medical services, and little knowledge on health. The citizens of developing countries have a low to medium standard of living because their per capita income is still developing, and their technological capacity is still being developed. There is also an unequal distribution of income in developing countries, and their factors of production are not fully utilized. Developing countries are also referred to as third-world countries or least-developed countries.

Countries are categorized according to their economic development. The United Nations classifies countries as developed, developing, newly industrialized or developed, and countries in transition such as Kazakhstan, Kyrgyztan, Turkmenistan, and the former USSR. The World Bank classifies countries according to their GNI per capita income: low income ($995 or less) and lower middle income ($996-$3,945); as developing countries with an upper middle income ($3,946-$12,195); and high income (above $11,906) as developed countries.

(3) The country citizen living of standard level

The classification of a country does not only depend on its income but also on other factors that affect how their citizens live, how their economies are integrated into the global system, and the expansion and diversification of their export industries. A developed country is one that has a high level of industrial development, bases its economy on technology and manufacturing instead of agriculture. The factors of production such as human and natural resources are fully utilized resulting in an increase in production and consumption which leads to a high level of per capita income. A country with a high Human Development Index (HDI) rating is considered a developed country. It not only measures the economic development and GDP of a country but also its education and life expectancy. A developed country's citizens enjoy a free and healthy existence.

The term "developed country" is synonymous to "industrialized country, post-industrial country, more developed country, advanced country, and first-world country." The United Kingdom, France, Germany, Canada, Japan, Switzerland, and the United States of America are only a few of those considered as developed countries.

A developing country, on the other hand, is one that has a low level of industrialization. It has a higher level of birth and death rates than developed countries. Its infant mortality rate is also high due to poor nutrition, shortage of medical services, and little knowledge on health. The citizens of developing countries have a low to medium standard of living because their per capita income is still developing, and their technological capacity is still being developed. There is also an unequal distribution of income in developing countries, and their factors of production are not fully utilized. Developing countries are also referred to as third-world countries or least-developed countries.

In conclusion, the measurement factors to decide whether the country is either developing or developed country. The factors depend on whether: whether the developed country is a country that has a high level of industrialization and per capita income while a developing country is a country that is still in the early stages of industrial development and has a low per capita income , whether the citizens of a developed country enjoy a free, healthy, and affluent existence while citizens of developing countries do not, whether the developed countries are also known as industrialized, advanced, and first-world countries while developing countries are also known as underdeveloped, least developed, and third-world countries. For example, The United States of America, Canada, Switzerland, Belgium, and France are examples of developed countries while India, Malawi, Honduras, the Philippines, and Rwanda are examples of developing countries as well as the infant mortality, birth, and death rates of developing countries are also higher compared to that of developed countries.

Why and how developed countries need
assist developing countries to develop

I think that we should help developing nations, But only to an extent. If we keep, And keep on giving them needs they will start to rely on foreign aid. I think charities are enough, But if the developing countries really need help then we give them help. But not too much, Basically they need to do something themselves and stop relying and take their own action. In exchange for our help maybe they could give us a bit of natural resources? Developing countries may need to be assisted, They may include these reasons:

- Global resource is shortage to allocate unfair challenge

Nowadays, global resources are not equally distributed in different countries. Thus, there are those who belong to the developed nations while there are others that belong to developing countries. With these unequal distribution, it is significant that developed countries must do their part in helping those who belong to the underprivileged sector. It is true that rich countries have their own problems to worry with; Can we introduce aquaponics in developing countries when they don't have the resources that first world countries have? In many areas, there is no electricity available that is needed for many aquaponics systems; developing countries require simplicity, reliability, and freedom from the need of grid powerhowever, it is still their responsibility to help the developing countries people need to solve resource can not be allocated fair problem, such as Afria is one developing country, many people are drinking drink water, due to drought , so they will not feel health and they will feel sick , even die. It is one example of natural resource of clean water shortage challenge to Afica. So, developed country, e.g. US , it has responsibilty to help African to drink clean water because clean water is allocated to supply to America people to drink in preference, due to global clean water supply is decreasing, but human number is increasing and clean water demand will also increase. If clean water is only supplied to US people to drink , even other developed countries people , they can drink the most clean water. The reason is because Africa people is poor or dirty or low education level or it is one developing country etc. factors to influence many African can not often drink any clean water. It is very unfair to this developing country.

In 2010, there were 925 million hungry people in the world; 19 million in developed countries, 37 million in Near East and North Africa, 53 million in Latin America and the Caribbean, 239 Million in Sub-Saharan Africa, and 578 million in Asia and the Pacific. This means that approximately 1 in 7 people are hungry. Protein- energy malnutrition is the most lethal form of malnutrition/hunger. It is a lack of calories and protein; protein is necessary for key bodily functions including provision of essential amino acids and the development and maintenance of muscles. Bringing aquaponics into third world countries would help prevent this problem by providing fish as a main source of protein. Poor nutrition is the cause or partial cause for at least half of the 10.9 million child deaths each year.

The number of hungry people has increased since 1997 due to three main problems: 1) neglect of agriculture relevant to very poor people by governments and international agencies; 2) worldwide economic crisis and 3) increase in food prices. Children who are poorly nourished suffer up to 160 days of illness each year. Malnutrition affects about 32% of children in developing countries. More than 70% of malnourished children live in Asia. Undernourished pregnant women in developing countries leads to 1 out of 6 infants born with low birth weight; this means higher neonatal death rates, increased occurrences of learning disabilities, mental retardation, poor health, blindness, and premature death.

There is enough food to provide everyone in the world with 2, 720 kilocalories per person per day, however many people don't have the land to grow or the money to buy the food they need for themselves and their children. 1 out of 3 people in developing countries are affected by vitamin and mineral deficiency.

So, I feel that aid has diverse results. It can both harm as well help development. Rich countries might be sidetracked in terms of focusing on programs that will spur development. Asian and African nations should create long-term plans that will reduce the dependency on aid, while rich countries should transition from traditional methods of giving support in new ways. Rich countries still argue on the premise that they cannot afford aid or that they are being over-generous. The main idea here is not that they are questioning the aid itself, but the development project. Rich countries must be on the poor countries aid as these people from poor nations face injustice and hardships that are often caused or increased by the programs and decision of rich nations themselves. However, giving aid is not really an act of generosity. Aid purchases things that donors desire. These might include political support in exchange for the "goodies" that the donor has provided. Rich countries must show support to the poor by abiding on the social, environmental aspects. It can also include adapting to climate change by changing one's own consumption. Another is to accept fairer trade rules. Moreover, rich countries can show true generosity by undergoing changes in the manner of living for the past few decades. It would be fair that rich countries believe they are being generous when they give out dole outs or loose change when poor people around the globe are trying to live on a few basics while living under the system that rich countries have developed. It is a reality that there are also poor people in rich countries that are undergoing tough times. However, it is not ethical to withdraw support from people abroad who are more underprivileged just because there are poor people in rich countries that need help as well.

In fact, many argue that the poor countries that rich countries provide financial aid are doing better economically. It is possible that these countries are growing and catching up with the standard of living. Say for example, the annual income of India might have greatly improved. However, when one divides that with the whole population, each Indian just obtains $3 or less per day. This issue requires obtaining the correct facts not only on financial aid, but on the act of generosity in this world. Rich countries do have a responsibility of giving to those developing country people's living need because they can enjoy any benefits in preference when resource is shortage and global need is also increasing in nowadays societies.

● Some developed countries have obligation to help developing countries

The rich have an obligation to help poor countries who were exploited by their colonial rulers. The United States had a head start with its vast natural resources. But many countries in Europe, such as Britain, became rich due to their colonial reign in Asia. They expanded their empire to include poor, resource-rich nations in Asia. They exploited the region's cheap labour, with workers getting little in return for their hard work. For Hong Kong , developing country and UK developed country. UK had obligation to help this developing country, HK before 1997.

Hong Kong was different though. Britain ruled Hong Kong for more than 150 years and I think both sides benefited. Today, the city is an international financial centre with a strong economy. But some countries did not benefit from colonial rule. For another example, IBM founder , Bill and Melinda Gates set up the Gates Foundation to help poor countries. We take a lot of things for granted. This cannot go on. A spirit of give-and-take is essential for world harmony. Developed countries may not be bound by law to help poor nations, but they have the responsibility - and the power - to do so.

However, developed countries should help less developed ones. But whether this is an obligation is a matter for debate. I believe the government of a country should be responsible for the well-being of its people. It is wrong to allow outsiders to influence the development of a country. This could lead to serious problems.

A developed country faces various difficulties when choosing who to help. First, its choice could leave a lot of people unhappy and damage its relationship with other countries. Second, allowing foreigners to have a significant influence on a nation could lead to negative consequences. Some donors do not have the best intentions. They could use their power for their own advantage. This could lead to corruption and financial loss in the less developed country. Third, a developing nation may become dependent on foreign aid. And some donors might charge a hefty interest for their financial assistance. This could pose a bigger headache than not receiving aid at all. Hence, rich countries have to be careful when helping poor nations. It involves a lot of politics so the rich have the right to choose the recipient and ensure the aid does not get into the wrong hands.

- Rich countries have responsibilites to assist global economy development or balance economy development

When global economy is unbalance developing. It will bring the damage of kindly cooperation relationship , e.g. export and import business activities to develop our global economy in success. For example, China and America themselve trade war will cause these both countries‘ GDP export and import income loss, even global economy will be recession. So, rich country, such as US has responsibility to assist developing country, such as Afria, China, Korea, Taiwan to help them to raise business competive effort and bring long term export and import business cooperation and create many factory jobs to China, Korea, Africa, Taiwan factory workers. Then, they can build kindly business cooperative relationship to bring global economy benefit in long term. Then, our global economy development will succeed more easily.

The first rational basis behind donating to poor countries is the notion that all men are equal. Some may radically oppose this concept, noting that their countries should solely invest its own efforts to remedy impoverished sectors of the population. Given the spread of poverty and homelessness, some have arrived to the conclusion that aiding other countries is not in our best interest. However, this could not be further from the truth. As member of the human race, we all occupy an equitable status as global citizens, and nothing can detract from this truth. Centralise your focus on the relative needs of your nation disregards the ailing needs of the developing world.

The second consideration simply poses the question of why not? Although wealthier, developed countries are plagued by their own respective incidences of poverty and lack of resources, developing countries suffer greatly, in terms of their accessibility to medical aid, vaccines, clean water, and a number of other amenities that are gravely understated in importance. With this said, we must venture beyond the bounds of our own comfort zones, and aid other countries because we are lavished with such a bounty in resources ourselves. Another indispensable benefit of aiding impoverished countries. Foreign diplomacy can significantly aid the national security of any nation. And providing aid to a poor county can ultimately benefit us, improving our perception in their eyes, a cultivating a certain level of civility and coexistence that breeds peace, instead of war. The fewer enemies that a particular nation has, the better.

The final reason is simple. We should empathize with other human beings. Every day, countless children succumb to curable disease, malaria and a number of other pathogens that could easily be treated with outside aid. Both children and adults are sold into slavery and trafficked around the world. Of course, the lingering issue of starvation is a palpable one that still plagues the world today. With this said, we should uphold a noble standard that permits forcign aid for this very reason. One often hears the argument that it is all very well to preach equity but given the planetary emergency the world faces from the threat of climate change we must set aside the equity principle in the interests of humanity as a whole. This is a wholly specious and self serving argument. It reflects the sense of entitlement to an affluent lifestyle, based on energy intensive production and consumption, while denying the even modest aspirations of people in developing countries.

For example, global climate changes to warmth challenge , it can cause developing countries people their health to be poor. In a densely interconnected and globalised world, it will be impossible to maintain islands of prosperity in an ocean of poverty and deprivation. It is not that developing countries are claiming the right to spew as much carbon as possible into the atmosphere without regard to the health of the planet. As the main victims of climate change– the impacts of which they are already suffering – they have a much bigger stake in dealing with this challenge. They are, in fact, doing much more than most developed countries, to adopt energy frugal methods of growth, conserving energy, promoting renewable power and limiting waste within the limits of their own resources.

Why and how developing countries people's poor health issue , it may influence developed countries businessmen income ? I shall indicate Africa , developing example , if African are health, then this country will have many workers to assist or help US businessmen to manufacture many products to sell to different countries in short time. If US businessmen hope to pay the low wage to reduce their long time expenditure, Afrian must need have health to do any hard jobs in factories. If US businessmen only feel Chinese workers can help them to do any low wage jobs in factories, when China have many new businesses develop to pay better wages to employ themselves Chinese workers. Then, many Chinese workers may choose to help themselves China employers to do the factory jobs to replace US employers. So, if US can help many African have health to work, it may bring uncounted long time benefits to US businesses. Hence, such as this case, it explains why rich people need to help developing countries to solve health challenge.

Methods developing countries can
become developed countries

- Main industries aspects need to develop

How can developing countries develop to be developed countries in success? What the difficulties to them , that they will need to solve in this development process ? In today's sophisticated society,people of the developing countries are still fighting for their basic righs such a better healthcare,proper education and a sound source of income.While the governments of the underdeveloped countries are struggling to improve the living standards of their people,I believe that contribution by richer nations should be more in this regard. To begin,all human beings should help each other.Govenments of richer nations can take many steps to improve the living standard of the poorer naions. I shall indicate these aspects that they need to concentrate on solving in order to achieve developed countries in success as below:

(1) Healthcare development

Firstly,in the field of healthcare,developed countries can support he underdeveloped in many ways.They can send their expert doctors to train the medical staff in the developing countries.Also,they can open free medical camps in the selected areas of poor countries.In this way free medical advice could be given.Such camps can also start health awarness compaigns to make people aware of unhealthy lifetyle. Moreover, experts from the developed countries can also help with the vaccination programmes in the developing countries.This will led to decrease in infant mortality rate.

(2) Educational development

Secondly,assistance in the field of education should be provide to the poorer nations.The developed countries can provide funds to open new schools and polytechnic institutions.These will not only increase the literacy rate,but will also provide vocational education.Furthermore,the rich governments should provide the students of poor countries an oportunity to study in the prestigious institutions by giving scholarships.This will promote poor people to gain higher education.

(3) Promoting free trade development

Finally,rich nations should help to improve the economy of poor countries.This can be done by promoting free trade.This wil reduce barriers to international trade such as tariff,import quotas and export fee and will help to lift the developing countries out of poverty. To conclude,if we want to live in a beter world with peace and harmony,we should always help each other.Therefore,I believe that richer nations should help the poor countries in all the fields.

● The challenges are needed to solve in development process

During the development process, they developing countries will need to solve these challenges, the developing or underdeveloped countries (as they were earlier named) are poor due to them having the following common characteristics as below:

The developing countries may have these social challenges , they need to solve , such as :

(1) On social medical aspect

Closed economy/State Controlled economy or practice of socialism (which is in practice -one man/one party dictatorship). Low levels of literacy and esp. female literacy (less than 75% female literacy). Low health and HDI indicators (corresponding to the literacy levels). Low per capita income. High incidence of corruption, nepotism and kleptocracy.

The following is the path chosen by most of the former “low income/under developed/poor nations” to become developed (Germany & Japan post WW2, South Korea, Taiwan, Brazil, South Africa and China - some are still in process)- Economically liberal but politically/socially conservative regimes. Immense government spending (Keynesian economics) on - Infrastructure (Roads, Schools, Bridges, Ports, Airports, Power Plants, Hospitals and primary health centers etc).

(2) On international trade social aspect

Opening up the economy to international trade and foreign investments. Export oriented manufacturing practices, wherein the bulk of the population which was in the primary sector (agriculture, animal husbandry and mining etc) shifts to the secondary sector (manufacturing) and experiences corresponding increase in wages/income.

Application of procedures and rule of law on a gradual basis from the earlier arbitrariness which reigned supreme. The first step, in my view, is to make sure to have an honest and capable government that are committed to the development of the country and to the welfare of all people in the country. It is, in fact, the most difficult step to start with. Once we have a good and capable government, it is not so difficult to figure out or implement all steps necessary to make the country developed and prosper. On the other hand, having a corrupt, incapable, in other words, not only dishonest, but also stupid and foolish government means losing everything, no matter how abundance resource your country has, or how much foreign assistance and aids your country receives.

However, some economists believe that they are not "developing", but MAINTAINED IN PERMANENT UNDERDEVELOPMENT on purpose. Market, same as everything, functions in 3D, the 3rd is the income strata. The "progress" is not for all the strata. Every upper stratum solves its own problems at expenses of pushing the next inferior one downwards (vertically) or over the edge (horizontally). Spend a few minutes on a search engine and you realize that the term "first world" is meaningless when referring to economic development. For example, Ireland, Switzerland and Sweden are examples of third world countries. A first world nation is one that allied with NATO as opposed to the Soviet Union during the Cold War.

(3) On solving social poverty aspect

Poverty is the default state of man. Knowledge is what allows us to go beyond our physical and cognitive limitations. With knowledge you can create technology that makes our lives better. At a base level, developing nations need a smaller percentage of their populations working in sustenance farming. This could be achieved by increases in farming productivity which would allow other people to specialize in making other goods and providing other services. Essentially creating more wealth.

Uaually, developing countries lack enough farming technology, they can't specialize in something other than sustenance farming if 80% of your population farms with oxen instead of machines. This is where knowledge comes in play. Many developing nations have rich natural resources and commodities they just don't have the knowledge necessary to turn it into something useful.

To summarize in one word what is necessary for a developing nation to become a developed one it is knowledge. Any one developing countries need to answer these questions, before they decide how to solve these social challenges in their development process as below:

What developing country will become the next developed nation? Why do they are developing countries ? How can they develop to be developed countries ? How long will it take for every country in the world to become developed? What is the way to develop a country? Which countries are likely to be developed countries soon?

For example, Brazilians is one developing country, because this country has high crime rate and poor rate is high and inflation is high. These are its social problems. As soon as hyperinflation and out-of-control crime was solved, Brazilians brought their money back to Brazil. The starting point for Brazilians is patriotism and nostalgia. Even with all the problems of corruption, taxes, bureaucracy and poor infrastructure if given a chance to make real money within the country a Brazilian will leave better opportunities in the US. So, Brazilians need to solve these social problems if this country hope to become one developed country in success. The easiest way to develop is: when each and every person decides to learn as much as possible, and decides to behave like civilized persons, who have total respect for all other persons' physical and patrimonial integrity. It's that easy and simple. But, often, the easiest things in life are the most difficult to learn.

- What a developing country should do to be a developed one?

The countries that developed the fastest often had the longest paths. If you compensate for that fact, then it becomes obvious that economic freedom is both necessary and sufficient. In particular, countries should avoid: socialism, i.e. collectivization of the means of production expropriation, i.e. robbing foreign investors of their properties autarchy, i.e. cutting all international trade. The less countries engage in these, the faster they develop.

● How can a developing country become a developed country? Well, you could study economic history and learn how the present developed countries attained their present positions. There are also several examples in real time: look at how China and India are moving their countries from third world countries to developed economies. Two other interesting examples: Several African countries are using primarily cell phone techologies for communication and bypassing the infrastructure requirements for hardline technology. Ireland is well know to have been deforested when it's forests were harvested for the coal and fuel requirements of industrializing.

● Developed Countries need to help Developing Countries to increase their competitive effort in societies

IMPROVEMENTS IN HEALTH, EDUCATION AND TRADE ARE ESSENTIAL FOR THE DEVELOPMENT OF POORER NATIONS. HOWEVER,THE GOVERNMENTS OF RICHER NATIONS SHOULD TAKE MORE RESPONSIBILITY FOR HELPING THE POORER NATIONS IN SUCH AREAS.

Eliminate political tension by encouraging participation of all in the political, constitutional and economic processes. I recommend developed countries, such as US, UK can help developing countries to develop in sucess in these several aspects:

-Invest in infrastructure, education and health care.

-Encourage rural agriculture by providing agricultural inputs and raising earned incomes.

-Raise levels of literacy

-Encourage the modern sectors of banking, manufacturing, retail,
and extractive industries,

-Provide adequate sanitation and clean water

-Open the countries to direct foreign investments

-Remove trade barriers to exports and imports.

-Reduce dependency on single sectors that is diversification .

Can bring global benefit when all countries are developed countries

1. How Globalization Affects Developed Countries

There are three perspective of globalization. Which are as : The Hyper globalist perspective: This says that economies are becoming Denationalized due to this government will lose it influence over the trade within its border. It will have both good and bad effects. The Skeptical perspective: it is kind based on myth that globalization will not help the under develop country as they do not perform a greater role in flow of trade and services in the global economy.

I assume that future one day, all countries can become developed countries. The globalization development effect will be caused by our global successful development. Does it means that globalization can only bring benefits ? I shall explain that when all countries can developed successfully. Globalization ought not only bring benefits to our global societies as below:

Globalization brings people and businesses together through the international exchange of money, ideas, and culture. However, some critics say it adversely affects developed countries. Opinions exist on both sides of the globalization debate. Proponents claim lower opportunity costs, producing positive growth, and reduced market volatility. At the same time, opponents decry the reduction of domestic job growth, cost of mismanagement to countries and the world, and the stagnation of wages.

Conflicting Globalization Views

U.S. President Donald Trump, for example, has been very vocal on his views of globalization and has taken a protectionist stance when it comes to free trade under agreements like the North American Free Trade Agreement (NAFTA), calling for higher taxes on imports and fewer multinational trade agreements. He has also increased tariffs on foreign goods to discourage their importation and use. No matter how much economists are quick to extol the universal benefits of globalization, some politicians and other economist demonize globalization as a force that takes away domestic jobs. These conflicting viewpoints have created a maelstrom of opinions and policies across developed countries that range from extreme protectionism through trade barriers, like President Trump's example, to complete openness.

From an economic standpoint, globalization is typically defined as the increase in the global trade of goods, services, capital, and technology. This growth in trade has been especially acute between developed countries like the United States and emerging markets, such as China. There are many factors behind the increase in global trade. European devastation after World War I and II helped to jumpstart America and an industrial superpower and exporter. Lower transportation costs have reduced the costs of trade, technologies have eliminated some barriers altogether, and liberal economic policies have helped lower political barriers to trade. While cost reductions have helped accelerate trade, the largest driver behind global trade is supply-demand economics and the desire to increase consumption on the part of both importers and exporters.

Benefits of globalization

The core benefit of globalization is the comparative advantage—that is, the ability of one country to produce goods or services at a lower opportunity cost than other countries. While the idea seems simple on the surface, it quickly becomes counterintuitive when examined more deeply. The theory suggests that two countries capable of producing two commodities at different costs can benefit the most by exporting the good where the comparative advantage exists. For example, a developing country may have a comparative advantage in producing cement, and the United States may have a comparative advantage in producing semiconductors. While the U.S. may be able to produce cement more efficiently than the developing country, the U.S. would still be better off focusing on semiconductors because of its comparative advantage. This is why globalization is powerful as a driver of global consumption between countries of all capabilities.

One of the major potential benefits of globalization is to provide opportunities for reducing macroeconomic volatility on output and consumption via diversification of risk. The overall evidence of the globalization effect on macroeconomic volatility of output indicates that although direct effects are ambiguous in theoretical models, financial integration helps in a nation's production base diversification, and leads to an increase in specialization of production. However, the specialization of production, based on the concept of comparative advantage, can also lead to higher volatility in specific industries within an economy and society of a nation. As time passes, successful companies, independent of size, will be the ones that are part of the global economy.

Empirical evidence suggests that a positive growth effect takes place in countries that are sufficiently rich when it comes to globalization. For investors and economies, globalization also provides the opportunity to reduce the volatility of output and consumption, since products and services can be imported or exported with greater ease. Fewer "bubbles" arise from a mismatch in supply and demand if the production of goods and services is more elastic. But, when all countries can develop to become developed countries, globalization developed countries which may also bring these disadvantages as below:

Drawbacks of globalization

Globalization is often criticized for taking away jobs from domestic companies and workers. After all, the U.S. cement industry will go out of business if imports from a developing country drive down prices, even if consumption increases. Small U.S. cement companies would find it difficult to compete and likely shut down, leaving workers unemployed, while the larger U.S. cement industry would likely experience a significant protracted decline.

A second criticism is the high cost of a comparative or absolute advantage to a country's own well-being if mismanaged. For example, China has become a leading worldwide emitter of carbon dioxide thanks to its comparative advantage in manufacturing a wide range of products. Other countries may have a comparative advantage in mining certain natural resources—such as crude

oil—and mishandle the revenue generated from those activities.
A final disadvantage of globalization is the increase in wages for workers, which can hurt corporate profitability. For example, if a rich country has a high comparative advantage in developing software, they may drive up the price of software engineers around the world, which makes it difficult for foreign companies to compete in the market.
The phenomenon of globalization began in a primitive form when humans first settled into different areas of the world; however, it has shown a rather steady and rapid progress in recent times and has become an international dynamic which, due to technological advancements, has increased in speed and scale, so that countries in all five continents have been affected and engaged.

What Is Globalization? Why and how globalization may achieve when global countries can develop to become developed countries ?

Globalization is defined as a process that, based on international strategies, aims to expand business operations on a worldwide level, and was precipitated by the facilitation of global communications due to technological advancements, and socioeconomic, political and environmental developments.
The goal of globalization is to provide organizations a superior competitive position with lower operating costs, to gain greater numbers of products, services, and consumers. This approach to competition is gained via diversification of resources, the creation and development of new investment opportunities by opening up additional markets and accessing new raw materials and resources. Diversification of resources is a business strategy that increases the variety of business products and services within various organizations. Diversification strengthens institutions by lowering organizational risk factors, spreading interests in different areas, taking advantage of market opportunities, and acquiring companies both horizontal and vertical in nature.
Industrialized or developed nations are specific countries with a high level of economic development and meet certain

socioeconomic criteria based on economic theory, such as gross domestic product (GDP), industrialization and human development index (HDI) as defined by the International Monetary Fund (IMF), the United Nations (UN) and the World Trade Organization (WTO). Using these definitions, some industrialized countries are: United Kingdom, Belgium, Denmark, Finland, France, Germany, Japan, Luxembourg, Norway, Sweden, Switzerland, and the United States.

Components of Globalization

The components of globalization include GDP, industrialization and the Human Development Index (HDI). The GDP is the market value of all finished goods and services produced within a country's borders in a year and serves as a measure of a country's overall economic output. Industrialization is a process which, driven by technological innovation, effectuates social change and economic development by transforming a country into a modernized industrial, or developed nation. The Human Development Index comprises three components: a country's population's life expectancy, knowledge and education measured by the adult literacy, and income.

The degree to which an organization is globalized and diversified has bearing on the strategies that it uses to pursue greater development and investment opportunities.

When all countries can become developed countries. They may bring the Economic Impact on Developed Nations as below: Globalization compels businesses to adapt to different strategies based on new ideological trends that try to balance the rights and interests of both the individual and the community as a whole. This change enables businesses to compete worldwide and also signifies a dramatic change for business leaders, labor and management by legitimately accepting the participation of workers and government in developing and implementing company policies and strategies. Risk reduction via diversification can be accomplished through company involvement with international financial institutions and partnering with both local and multinational businesses.

Globalization brings reorganization at the international, national and sub-national levels. Specifically, it brings the reorganization of production, international trade and the integration of financial markets. This affects capitalist economic and social relations, via multilateralism and microeconomic phenomena, such as business competitiveness, at the global level. The transformation of production systems affects the class structure, the labor process, the application of technology and the structure and organization of capital. Globalization is now seen as marginalizing the less educated and low-skilled workers. Business expansion will no longer automatically imply increased employment. Additionally, it can cause a high remuneration of capital, due to its higher mobility compared to labor.

The phenomenon seems to be driven by three major forces: the globalization of all product and financial markets, technology, and deregulation. Globalization of product and financial markets refers to an increased economic integration in specialization and economies of scale, which will result in greater trade in financial services through both capital flows and cross-border entry activity. The technology factor, specifically telecommunication and information availability, has facilitated remote delivery and provided new access and distribution channels, while revamping industrial structures for financial services by allowing entry of non-bank entities, such as telecoms and utilities.

When all countries can become developed countries. In a global economic view, power is the ability of a company to command both tangible and intangible assets that create customer loyalty, regardless of location. Independent of size or geographic location, a company can meet global standards and tap into global networks, thrive and act as a world-class thinker, maker, and trader, by using its greatest assets: its concepts, competence, and connections. When all developing countries become developed countries, they may bring these beneficial effects as below:

Some economists have a positive outlook regarding the net effects of globalization on economic growth. These effects have been analyzed over the years by several studies attempting to measure the impact of globalization on various nations' economies using variables such as trade, capital flows, and their openness, GDP per capita, foreign direct investment (FDI) and more. These studies examined the effects of several components of globalization on growth using time-series cross-sectional data on trade, FDI and portfolio investment. Although they provide an analysis of individual components of globalization on economic growth, some of the results are inconclusive or even contradictory. However, overall, the findings of those studies seem to be supportive of the economists‘ positive position, instead of the one held by the public and non-economist view.

Trade among nations via the use of comparative advantage promotes growth, which is attributed to a strong correlation between the openness to trade flows and the effect on economic growth and economic performance. Additionally, there is a strong positive relation between capital flows and their impact on economic growth. Foreign Direct Investment's impact on economic growth has had a positive growth effect in wealthy countries and an increase in trade and FDI, resulting in higher growth rates.8 Empirical research examining the effects of several components of globalization on growth, using time series and cross-sectional data on trade, FDI and portfolio investment, found that a country tends to have a lower degree of globalization if it generates higher revenues from trade taxes. Further evidence indicates that there is a positive growth-effect in countries that are sufficiently rich, as are most of the developed nations.

The World Bank reports that integration with global capital markets can lead to disastrous effects, without sound domestic financial systems. One of the potential benefits of globalization is to provide opportunities for reducing macroeconomic volatility on output and consumption via diversification of risk.

However, when all countries can become developed countries, they may also bring these harmful effects as below:

Non-economists and the wide public expect the costs associated with globalization to outweigh the benefits, especially in the short-run. Less wealthy countries from those among the industrialized nations may not have the same highly-accentuated beneficial effect from globalization as more wealthy countries, measured by GDP per capita, etc. Although free trade increases opportunities for international trade, it also increases the risk of failure for smaller companies that cannot compete globally. Additionally, free trade may drive up production and labor costs, including higher wages for a more skilled workforce, which again can lead to outsourcing jobs from countries with higher wages. Moreover, domestic industries in some countries may be endangered due to comparative or absolute advantage of other countries in specific industries. Another possible danger and harmful effect is the overuse and abuse of natural resources to meet new higher demands in the production of goods.

In overall, when all countries can develop to become developed countries, they may bring these general benefits to influence our society to bring positive changes. They may include: Globalization activity doesn't only reduce trade boundary but it lot more effects like one country come closer to the economy of other country, it help in mixture of culture, it helps in transfer information and technology, increase group of buyer and seller of products and services etc. this are only few advantages of globalizations. Due to globalization trade is getting more interdependent and to protect interest of every nation W.T.O keep a close look over the trade of every nation. Due globalization many environmental threats are evolved every country is moving toward industrialization which increase global warming and it is needed to be checked. Social problem are also occurred like exploitation of labour, increase in child labour in developing nations, lack of powerful labour union etc this social problem are needed to taken care of and proper law should be made to avoid such kind of problems. As every things as has some advantages, it also has some disadvantages also.

Advantages:

- New market for product.
- Helps in growth of economy.
- Increase in infrastructure.
- Free flow of technology and information.
- Reduction in poverty.
- Increases in employments.
- International body governs trade through its law, so interest of every country should be protected.

Disadvantages are as follows:

- It brings competitions because of which small scale industries suffer in under develop countries.
- Globalization lead to growth in infrastructure but on other hand it bring harm to environment due to industrialization, reduction in forest areas.
- Due to globalization environment, labour, resource of under develop countries are exploited by develop countries.
- Poor trade union.
- Lack of control over country economy by its governments.

Effect of globalization on developing countries or third world countries

The thinking of first world, second world and third world countries are given by U.S.A which place itself as the first world nation, European countries as second world nations and as far as third world country are concerned under develop and developing countries come under this categories. The third world countries are further classified as under developed countries and developing countries. In under developed, countries like Afghanistan, Nepal, Bangladesh, Nigeria, Bhutan, Pakistan etc comes this are the growing nations but as far as development of economy is concerned they are far behind. In developing countries, countries like China, India, South Africa, Brazil etc are included because this are among fastest growing nation after globalization has taken place. But under develop countries are not much benefited because of this globalization process. Rather than getting benefit they are exploited. In a sense, due to cheap labour these countries manpower is exploited and it natural resource is been taken away as we can take the example of china, china is investing a lot in African nation and on exchange of this it is utilizing its natural resources.

What influences to the countries like china and India has grown tremendously after globalization.

Before globalizations export of china was not very high but now it is one the global leader in exports and as far as India is concerned before India was accounted only for 0.6 % of world export and now it is accounted for 1 % of world exports. Brazil has also show huge growth its per capita income has also increased. Countries like Bhutan, Malaysia, Indonesia etc has tremendous growth in GDP in past five years. Outsourcing has increased in these nations. Now India earns 51% of GDP from service sectors and its service sector is growing tremendously because of it excellence in IT sectors and this boosted up after globalizations. Now china earns major part of it GDP from export which increased after globalization. As far as Latin America is concerned Brazil has show tremendous growth in export, technology and manufacturing sectors. And now it is among top five of developing nations.

Effect of globalization on developed countries when all developing countries can become developed countries

Due to globalization the develop countries are moving towards underdeveloped countries like India, China, Indonesia etc for outsourcing their job to these countries because of cheap labour. Nowadays develop nation are coming to under develop nation for setting up manufacturing plants in these nation because of its availability of cheap and skilled labours. Due to globalization develop countries are facing intense competition from underdeveloped countries, competition in sense employment, exports, technology etc. Due to globalization developed countries are also exploit resources like natural resource, manpower, and environment etc. of underdeveloped nations. Also, due to globalization the dominance of developed nation is also reducing. The people of developed nation are facing intense competition for job from people growing nation like china, India, Thailand etc. now for FDI in developed nation are reducing due increase in the FDI in developing countries like china, Brazil, India etc. Thus, when all developing countries can develop to become developed countries in future one day. Globalization developed countries got new market for their products and services, and new place for their business expansions.

Development of "Regional economic" will truly help India to build viable economic future for its citizens.

Due to globalization various effect and development has take place which help india to build viable economic future for its citizens. Due Globalization to this the infrastructure of India has developed a lot because of which transportation, sanitary, hygiene, sports complex and stadium has developed a lot and still developing which will give better environment for future generation. Nowadays, foreign education institutes are coming to india which has increased the level of education. Export of india is increasing with each quarter which help to reduce the fiscal deficit and increase the GDP of the nation.

Nowadays more and more manufacturing industries are established because of which more employment is created and hence improving per capita income of the nation. Due globalization India is more concerned about the global warming and planning its growth in such a way that it could reduce it contribution in global. And it will be helpful for future citizens.

Regional economies help to reduce domination of developed economies on the developing economies.

Developments in regional economy will strength the self reliability of the nation which will help to reduction in the dependence on other nation. Development of regional economy will lead to increase in GDP, Standard of living, Per capita income of the nation. If India wants to emerge as supper power it has to develop it regional because it is the stepping stone toward it.

In conclusion, when all countries can develop to achieve developed countries. They will create development of regional economy to our global societies. Then, they may bring these benefits in possible. They may include: Development of regional economy will lead to reduce in inequalities of distribution of wealth, development of regional economy will lead to increase in metropolitan culture, development of regional economy will lead increase the contributions of every state in Indian GDP, development of regional economy will lead to reduction of poverty, unemployment and illiteracy.

2. Economic growth advantages and disadvantages

When all developing countries can develop to be developed countries, then it may also bring global economic growth. However, I believe that when global societies can have sudden economic growth in short time, due to all or many developing countries can develop to be developed countries in success. They may bring advantages and disadvantages both aspects as below:

Economic development can be describe as the development of economic wealth of countries or regions for the well-being of their inhabitants such as the improvement and innovation on the political, economic, and social of its people. Economic development and growth are totally different in terms which are used in economics. Economic development refers to economic growth which accompanied by changes in economic structure and output distribution. So, economic growth may be necessary but not sufficient to attain economic development. Thus, peoples always said that economic development is the problems of underdeveloped countries and economic growth to those of developed countries. Underdeveloped countries always face some problems such as low income, weakness of human resource and also the economic vulnerability. These problems also made the countries hard to attain the development of economic. However, for those developed countries, they do not face the same problems as what underdeveloped countries do, therefore, they are more easily to attain the economic development and treat it as an economic growth.

In addition, in the term of economic development is much more comprehensive because it implies progressive changes in the socio-economic structure of a country. Nowadays, the evolution of new technology is directly related to economic development. Without high technology in a country, it is hard to bring an economic development toward its people. Viewed in this way economic development involves a steady decline in agricultural shares in GNP and continuous increase in shares of industries, trade banking construction and services. However, economic growth just only refers to the rise in total output in a country; development implies change in technological and institutional organization of production as well as in distributive pattern of income. Hence, if compared to the goal of development, economic growth is much easy to realize. Between, we just need a larger mobilization of resources and raising their productivity by enhance it to be more efficiency and effective, then the output level can be raised and economic growth will occur. However, the development process is far more extensive than the economic growth. Not only a rise in output, it also involved changes in composition of output, and shift in the allocation of productive resources, and reduction or elimination of poverty, inequalities and unemployment. However, economic development is impossible without having an economic growth but economic growth is possible without an economic development. Growth is just increase in GNP but it does not have any other parameters to it; unlike development which can be conceived as Multi-Dimensional process.

Are economic growth and development worthwhile?

Economic growth and development have their advantages and also disadvantages. Although economic growth widens the range of human choices, but this may not necessarily bring happiness toward people. Happiness is dependent on the relationship between wants and resources. People may become more satisfied, not only by having more wants met, but perhaps also by renouncing certain material goods. Wealth may make people less happy if it increases wants more than resources. Furthermore, acquisitive and achievement-oriented societies may be more likely to give rise to

individual frustration.
Advantages
Economic growth will decreases famine, starvation, infant mortality, and death; gives us greater leisure; can enhance art, music, and philosophy; and gives us the resources to be humanitarian. Economic growth will especially benefit to societies in which political desire exceed the resources, because it may prevent what might otherwise prove to be social tension that people can't take it. However, without economic growth, the desires of one group can be met when others expense on it. Lastly, economic growth can help newly independent countries in mobilizing resources to increase the power of a nation.

Disadvantages
Growth has its value. First, the disadvantage might be the acquisitiveness, materialism, and dissatisfaction with one's present state associated with a society's economic struggles. Second, liquidity, objective, and self-associated with economic growth may undermine the reliance on extended family system, in fact, the focus of the prevailing social structure. Third, economic growth, which depends on the rational and technological innovation and changes in scientific methods, often is the threat in religious and social authority. Fourth, economic growth often require more specialized work, which may be caused by more objective, accompanied more drab and monotonous tasks, more discipline, and a pair of process loss.
In addition, economic growth which follow by large organizational units are more likely to lead to bureaucratization, objective, communication problems, and the use of force were consistent. Economic growth and development of large enterprises with a manufacturer's products and services while demand increased, and urban growth, this may be is accompanied byrootlessness, environmental blight disease, and unhealthy living conditions, even in the narrow social values change and may ultimately lead to a new dynamic equilibrium that is better than the old static equilibrium,

the transition could have some very painful issues. In addition, the political transformation, as rapid economic growth, may lead to greater concentration, stress, social disruption, even authoritarian. Therefore, even if the population seriously committed to economic growth, its implementation is not likely at all costs pursued. All societies must take into account that the conflicts with the maximization of economic growth and other objectives. Because it was want sits in high level positions, a developing country own citizens can promote the local production control to reduce the growth in the short term.

The question now is what will be weighed to achieve an orderly, stable society, and maintain traditional values and culture, and promoting political autonomy? Economic growth is the increase a country's per capita output. Economic development, economic growth has resulted in the poorest strata of the population or level of education, changes to improve the output distribution of economic welfare and economic changes in different structures.

Economic growth and development of Asia when all or many developing countries can develop to be developed countries

Nowadays, economic development in Asia shows high impact of economic development of this respective continent. Economy of Asia has taken an important part in the view of the world's economy. These continents have adopted one of the following economic systems such as capitalism, socialism, communism, and fascism. As we know, Asia is the largest continent in terms of area surface and also the population. Beside it, it is also the region with the highest growth rate. Below are Asian countries that contribute their economic development to our society.

Of all the Asian Countries, the only Asian country included among the industrialized countries is Japan. According to the International Monetary Fund, the country per capita was GDP 32,608 U.S. dollars or in 2009, the 23$^{rd}$ highest on record. Moreover, according to certain criteria, the term means that developed countries is the countries that having a high level of development. What standards and which countries are classified as being developed, is a controversial issue which surrounded by a fierce debate. Thus, economic criteria tend to dominate discussions. Countries which having per capita income and high per capita gross domestic product (GDP) will be described as developed countries. Another criterion is the industrialization; countries in the tertiary and quaternary sector-of industry leading will be described as development. Another recent measure, the human development index, which combines economic measures, and other measures of national income, life expectancy and education indicators, have become prominent. This criterion will define the development country as those very high (HDI) rating. However, many exceptions exist when the decision to "developed country" status is used to measure the subject. Countries do not fit this definition are classified as developing countries.

However, Taiwan, Hong Kong and Singapore are regarded as newly industrialized countries. The category of newly industrialized country (NIC) is a socioeconomic classification which applied to various countries in the world by political scientists and economists. NIC is the nation's economy has not yet reached first world status, but in the macro sense, the development of the countries is normally faster than counterpart. Another feature of newly industrialized countries is that undergoing in rapid economic growth (usually export-oriented). However, the starting or ongoing industrialization is an important indicator of NIC. In many newly industrialized countries, may also be experiencing social unrest by major primary rural, or agricultural, populations migrate to the cities, where the thousand of laborers can be draw by growth of manufacturing concerns and factories. In the social development process, it usually shares some characteristic such as increased social freedoms and civil rights, strong political leadership, which switch from an agricultural to an industrial economy, the other common features, especially in the manufacturing sector, an increasingly open market economy with free trade and other heavy capital investment from countries around the world. In addition, the political leadership in their area of influence and lastly is they have lowered poverty rates.

I shall indicate China, Philippines, India, North Korea these developing country when they can become developed country , what it can bring global social change influence example. Moreover, as we know, the history and culture of China is their secret to improve their economy, even if it ruled and control by their state. Prior to 1979, China maintained a centrally planned or command economy. The economy of China with the large proportion is directed by the state which established production goals, controlled prices, distribution, and most of the economic control of resources. During the 1950s, all of China's individual household farms were collectivized into large communes. To support rapid industrialization, the central government starts to take large-scale physical and human capital investment during 1960-1970s. As a result, by 1978, nearly three quarters of industrial production generated by the central control of state-owned enterprises according to centrally planned output targets. Private enterprises and foreign invested enterprises are almost non-existent.

A central objective of Chinese government was to make China's economy relatively self-sufficient. Foreign trade was generally limited to those commodity which unable to obtain or receive the goods in China. The Government's policy to keep the Chinese economy relatively stagnant and inefficient, mainly because of where the profits of some enterprises and farmers to stimulate competition, in fact, does not exist, price and production controls caused widespread economic distortions. China's standard of living is much lower than those of many other.

In addition, India is contributing in business process outsourcing improvement for the information technology which has a significant impact for the economic development in South Asia. The Philippines is improving, because they help to remittances from abroad, they send money to their loved ones from overseas Filipino workers to improve their country. North Korea shows hammer and sling as a symbol for their communistic views of their economic system in Far East Asia. While South Korea shows modern technology that is influence from Western countries which results an improvement of technology in their designated countries. Indonesia is a Muslim country, the whole of Asia's largest population by the Dutch colony. It is based on their banking and finance in the Islamic way of life. This is also the case in Malaysia was a British colony.

After analyze the information of some Asian Countries, I discovered that they are facing several problems in economic development. First, they have low standard of living, low level of production, there is a rapid population growth, they having a high rate of unemployment, lastly, there are over dependence on agricultural production and exportation of raw materials and also the international trade.

Economic growth and development of Malaysia

According to the recent The Star's newspaper, Malaysia economic development is one of fastest and steady in global economic scenario. Malaysia GDP per capita has been estimated to be $15,700 in fiscal year 2008. This is a clear indication of tremendous economic development in Malaysia. Malaysia economy is a middle income country that has developed since 1970's. It was previously a mere raw materials producing economy, which has evolved now as a developing multi-sector economy. This growth bears testimony to impressive economic development at Malaysia. Prime Minister Abdullah, after coming to power in 2003, has tried to develop economy of this south Asian country by introducing value added production. He took a number of measures to introduce hi-tech technologies and encouraged investments in high technology industries, medical technology and pharmaceuticals. Efforts have been made by government of Malaysia to stop its dependence on export products. However, exports of electronics goods have always been a major factor in Malaysia economy. There has been huge profit accrued from export of oil and gas and it has been a major factor for Malaysia economic development. There have been huge profits from high energy prices, although there was high cost of gasoline and diesel fuel. This, however, made Kuala Lumpur minimize financial assistance of government. It has been found that currency value of Malaysia has hiked 6 percent per year when pitted against dollar in fiscal years 2006 to 2008.

Model of economy development: The production function how can be influenced to change when many or all developing countries can become developed countries

In macroeconomics, the production function is a function which specifies combination of all input from the output. In the macro-economy, production functions are functions that determine the output of a company which entered all combinations of input. A meta-production function comparing the practices of companies that has to change input to output to determine the function of the most efficient production practices of the entity that is, whether the most efficient production practices that qualify or production practices that are actually the most efficient. In these cases, the maximum output production process technology is defined as mathematical function of one or more entered. In other words, given a collection of all technical combination allows the output and input, just include a combination of maximum output for a given set of inputs to the production or function. Production function can be defined as specification of minimum input requirements needed to produce a total output that was, by given current technology. It is usually assumed that the production of unique functions can be built for every production technology.

Assuming when many or all developing countries can develop to become developed countries in future one day, they may bring these influences to our social technologic production function changes as below:

The maximum output possible from the set of technology inputs of all, the economic use in the production function analysis is the abstract essence of the technical and managerial problems associated with a specific production process. Engineering and managerial problems of technical competence is assumed to be broken, so the analysis can focus on the problem of efficiency allocate. States are assumed to make choices about how much each input of allocate factors put to use and how much output to produce, remember the cost (purchase price) of each factor, the sale price of output, and the factors represent technology to determine its production function. Frame results in one or more constant input can be used, for example, capital can be assumed to be fixed (constant) in the short term, and labor and possibly other variables such as input raw material, while in the long run, the quantity of capital and the factors that can be made by the company are variable. In the long term, companies may even have the choice of technology, represented by the various functions of production as possible.

Input to output relationship is non-financial, that the production function relating physical inputs to physical outputs, and prices and the cost is reflected in the function. But the production function is not a complete model of the production process: intentionally abstract from the inherent aspects of physical production process that some would consider extremely important, including error, entropy or waste. In addition, the production functions do not typically model business processes, well, ignoring the role of management. (For primer on the basic elements of the production of Microeconomics theory, see production theory policies).

The main purpose of the production function is to address allocate efficiency in the use of input factors in production and distribution of factory income such factors. Based on certain assumptions, the production function can be used to reduce a marginalized product for each factor, which implies an ideal division of the revenue generated from the output to the income from their every input factor of production.

How global developed economy influences household expenditure decision?

In the saving function, there is a mathematical relation between saving and income by the household sector. Thus, the saving function can be stated as an equation such as a simple linear equation or a diagram indicated as the saving line. This function captures the relationship between savings and income, one of the other sides the relationship between consumer incomes, constitutes a cornerstone of Keynesian economics. The two key function to save the parameters are intercept, which indicates that self-saving, side slope, which is the marginal propensity to save, show that the induced savings. The injection- leakage model used in Keynesian economics is based on the saving function.

Saving function on Keynesian economics is the starting point for determination of equilibrium output injection, leakage model. It captures the household sector in which the relationship between savings and income. As the income for either consumption or savings to use, saving feature is the complementary consumption function. Reflects the fundamental psychological law put forward by John Maynard Keynes, consumer spending (and saving by the household sector) depends on the income and just some of the revenue is used for consumption and saving the rest. This function is presented either as a mathematical formula, usually as a simple linear equation, graph or savings line. In either form, income is a measure of disposable income, national income and GDP. However, the saving function makes it easy to divide saving into two basic types such as the autonomous saving and Induced saving. Autonomous saving is the intercept term. Induced saving is the slope. Lastly, the slope of marginal propensity to save (MPS) also considered as saving function

How global developed economy influences the labor supply function changes ?

In mainstream economic theory, labor supply is the total number of hours number of a workers want to work in a given real wage rate. From the diagram above, we can see the positive relationship between the wages rate and also the quantity of labor. When the wage rate is low, the quantity of the labor also is low. However, when there is a rose in wage rate will also increase the quantity of labor. Realistically, the labor supply is the role of various factors within an economy. For example, as a heavy increased of population will make downward pressure on wages which may lead to high unemployment.

How global developed economy influences wage rate versus labor leisure changes?

Labor supply curves are derived from the 'labor-leisure' trade-off. More hours worked earn higher incomes but necessitate a cut in the amount of leisure that workers enjoy. Therefore, there are two aspects, to provide the necessary amount of labor is due to changes in real wage rates. For example, the real wage rate raises the opportunity cost of leisure increases as the diagram shows above. This tends to cause workers to supply more labor (the "substitution effect"). However, as the real wage rate rises, workers earn a higher income for a given number of hours. If leisure is a normal good – the demand for it increases as income increases – this increase in income will tend to cause workers to supply less labor (the "income effect"). If the "substitution effect" is stronger than the "income effect" then the labor supply curve will be upward sloping and vice versa.

However, from the view of Marxist, a labor supply is a core requirement in a capitalist society. In order to avoid Labor shortage and ensure a labor supply, a large portion of the population must not possess sources of self-provisioning, which would allow them to be independent, and they must instead be compelled, in order to survive, to sell their labor for a subsistence wage.

Economic development theories: Harrod-Domar theory

When all or many countries can develop to be developed countries, how they can influence global technological growth rate changes. The Harrod-Domar theory delineates a functional economic relationship in which the growth rate of gross domestic product (g) depends directly on the national saving ratio (s) and inversely on the national capital/output ratio (k) so that it is written a g = s / k. The equation takes its name from a synthesis of analyses of growth process by two economists (Sir Roy Harrod of Britain and E.V. Domar of the USA). The Harrod-Domar model in the early postwar times was commonly used by developing countries in economic planning. With a target growth rate, the required saving rate is known. If the country is not capable of generating that level of saving, a justification or an excuse for borrowing from international agencies can be established. An example in the Asian context is to ascertain the relationship between high growth rates and high saving rates in the cases of Japan and China. It is more difficult to introduce the third building block of a growth model, the labor and population element. In the long run, growth rate is constrained by population growth and also by the rate of technological change.

● Climate change will impact developed countries to continue develop

Will developed countries become
developing countries

● Why does illness can cause global economic recession to developed countries

Firstly, I shall explain why unpredicted illness factor can cause developed countries' economic recession. Although developed countries have advantages and let people to believe that their any medical, economic, education, business etc. different industries aspects are developed in mature. Their these any industries aspects are better or are improved better to compare the developing countries. But, in fact, whether it is possible that their any industries aspects will become worse to compare developing countries when they do not continue to improve any one of their industries aspects. I shall indiate whether what factors my cause developed countries to become developing countries in possible.
Many developing countries are facing problem very different from that of the developed countries. Countries such as Japan, Germany are facing depleting population whether on the other side countries like India, Indonesia are facing severe resource crunch due to population explosion. In such situation measuring the progress of the countries on the same scales decided by developed industrialized world is injustice to these countries. Developed world have achieved there parameters after journey of around

200-250 years post industrialization while many developing countries are in their 60s-70s after getting freedom from crutches of colonialism. In such cases developing countries should formulate their own parameters for growth and development and continue their progress. So, it seems that any developing countries will have possible to develop to be better any developed countries. Otherwise, any developed countries will have possible to bring worse development when they have many people loss jobs. For example, US economy will go down nowadays, due to the Chinese serious illness influences many US people die. Many US businessmen can not continue to manufacture or sell their products because many people can not go to offices or factories to work. They need to stay at homes to avoid the illness attacks when they need to contact the illness people in workplace, or they are walking on streets, or they are catching any public transport. So,although US is one developed country, but it can not still to avoid this China illness attack. It is possible due to US government neglects to consider this China illness is one kind of death sick to cause US has many people to die easily in this year 2020. If US government can prohibit to let Chinese travellers to enter its country when China has occurred this serious illness caused in 2019 last year. These Chiness illness people can not enter US to cause this kind of illness to attack any US people lung to cause they die. After it is possible that US can avoid to cause many US people to die. So, it does not consider whether the country is developed or not to avoid global economic recession, because it is illness factor to cause developed countries' economic recession, such as US, UK nowadays economic recession.

- Increasing social crime rate and government assistance may cause developed countries to become developing coutries

Secondly, I shall explain why increasing social crime rate or many young people do criminal behaviors in society, it can influence developed countries to develop worse or can not develop better in its society. Otherwise, when on developing countries have less crime rate or decreases its crime rate, it can develop better or improve its society to be better. For a developing country to catch up to a developed country, it must not only grow, but grow faster than the developed country. While It is possible for such accelerated growth to occur through rapid industrialization, but there are many country-specific factors that directly affect a developing country's ability to catch up to developed countries. They range from growth of productivity, labour force participation rate, standard of living, infrastructure, political environment etc.

For example, when the developing country can improve its education quality to let many young people learn any kinds of new knowledge to like do any kinds of jobs, even, driving , factory labor, waitors, etc. low educational level jobs in society. Then, it will reduce its crime rate when many young people feel need to work. They won't need government to assist their life. Consequently, it will have possible to develop its economy or improve its economy to be better. In education primarily is the most essential quality that helps to empower the people of the country to communicate and achieve a common objective and is thus an extremely important driver for the developing to developed country journey. This is a common observation in all the developing countries. The one area that is still a struggle is education. Also, lack of education leads to increased poverty and disparity of income which leads to the $2^{nd}$ most hindrance in a countries journey to achieve a developed nation status. Maybe if the path chosen is that of streamlining lack of education, poverty, a more driven and focused effort with individuals who know and can fathom the importance of this change working towards achieving a developed nation status can be undertaken. A semi-industrial, pro-human development approach should be a path adopted to see a qualitative shift in reducing this gap.

All through our education we have learnt 'India is a developing country' which brings to thought, will it ever be recognized as a 'developed country'? And what is the criteria to qualify as a developed nation? Are these criteria set by the developed nations to meet their convenience? If this is the case it would be more logical for developing nations to set their own criteria. It gets very difficult for developing nations to meet the criteria set by the giant economies, as even a single step gone wrong could ruin the effort of years. India can be seen as an example, where the step of demonetization and GST together led to a growth rate of 5.7%, weakest growth rate since the first quarter of 2014. These steps would probably have a positive effect in the long run and it is worth the wait. Another question to bring our attention to is, are the developed countries developed in the true sense? Considering the parameter of crime rate, USA has a very high crime rate. Another aspect could be unemployment, again US has a good percent of unemployed individuals every year. So, aren't the developed nations also falling short? It may be a good strategy for developing nations could be establishing a path which would help them use their resources aptly and generate output for their people.

In this race of matching with the developed nations we are leading nowhere, better we set a different goal all together. Every nation has a different potential given different kinds of resources they possess hence expecting the same output from all makes little sense. Hope the coming generation gets to learn, 'India is a developed country in the true sense'. Hence, high crime rate, such as US has high crime rate. Because it has many young people do not like to work, they depend on government assistance. Then, any kinds of low skill or low educational level job employers will feel difficult to find them to work. Then, their society will cause low skillful labour shortage challange. It is not due to US lacks enough low skill or low educational workers, it is due to they do not like to work, they fccl wages are less , when their government can give any money or loss job allowance to support their lives in long time. It can enough these low educational level or low skillful level young people choose not work. Then, this US developed country will not have any young people to do any service job, e.g. driving public transport, waiter, security. When these kinds of job old people need to retire, these employers can not find any young people to replace them to do these service jobs. They can only choose to employ another old age people to replace the retired service staffs. Then, these kinds any one of service jobs can not raise their service level, their service performance will be worse or keep the same service level, it means that their performance can not perform better level to serve their clients in US society. It implies that developed country, such as US its general social service level will be worse or they can not be improved to satisfy their client needs. In this developed country's poor service environment, how to explain it can still keep its developed country's position , such as US.

However, it may bring the question -Will Developing Countries ever catch up with Developed Countries? will remain unanswered because you have rightly pointed out that leaders of developing countries have given up on the economy and they keep themselves busy with other matters. Political institutions has great impact on the development of a nation. Industrial revolution happened in England instead of any other country because England had the best political institution that time. We have been hearing that if the 20$^{th}$ century belonged to developed countries of North America and Europe then 21$^{st}$ century will be of developing countries such as India, China and Brazil. But development is the crucial word which draws boundary between two countries-developed or developing. According to the World Bank reducing poverty is the main purpose of the development. After the World War 2, many nations have had significant growth however only few have been able to catch up with developed countries in terms of per capita income. From 1940s till 1990s poor countries grew slowly, falling farther behind to rich ones in income. Only few countries such as South Korea and Singapore were able to gain rich status. Since 2000, developing nations such as India and China are economically growing and managing growth rates of above 10% per year. With such continuous growth rates, developing nations can converge with developed nations and that would mean higher standard of living and good economic and political power. But this growth is limited to few countries since many countries still have not opened their domestic market to international markets. These countries also have barriers in technology and availability and allocation of resources. So, it seems that developing countries still need more time to develop exceed to the developed countries because they, such as China, Korea, Taiwan , Singapore etc. have poor technology and shortage of allocation or resource to compare the developed countries, such as US, UK etc. even their crime rate may reduce or many young people may accept to do the low skillful or low education level service jobs in societies.

- Developed countries lack effort to manufacture cheap products to sell strengths

Hence, we need to look at every economy as a company and developing a unique selling proposition becomes relevant. The United States has a USP of being the most technologically advanced and productive country. China has managed to become an exporter of cheap goods, the United Kingdom till now was a financial hub- there are chances of that changing thanks to BREXIT with the rise of Dublin. When we look at developing economies, such as India, we do not see any USP in the making. What is India's USP? I cannot think of any. People talk about demographic dividend to India in terms of a large young population. Such a population, which is largely uneducated is a demographic curse. Merely being a large market for goods and services is a bad idea for a USP. Developing countries need to introspect sometimes to look at the systemic challenges that they face. Looking towards developed economies is not always the best alternative. Such as China can choose to buy cheap product, because its technologic developement is poor. It is its strength to manufacture cheap products to sell to overseas to earn foreign income and raise GDP on export aspect. So, China may have much development chance to grow up its economy when it can decide which kinds of cheap or easier manufacturing products to sell to overseas when these countries can not supply from themselves manufactures, they need to buy from China in long time.

While the share of many western economies remained very low. However, over the years the trend started to reverse and many western countries have now become very developed while third world countries like India, China etc. continue on their journey from being developing to developed. We are currently a 2 trillion dollar economy and the eighth largest economy in the world. By 2030, India is predicted to be the fifth largest economy in the world. On purchasing power basis, India is the second largest economy in the world only behind China. Despite so many bright spots, we are faced with the paradox of being an advanced economy and still being one of the poorest in the world.

Otherwise, many such countries who are highly rich in natural resources continue to be plundered by the developed economies. Many countries continue to be haunted by the choices they made in past and turnaround being highly unlikely. They are often not helped by the injustices meted out by the developed economies who continue to take decision in their own self-interest. I feel the time has come when all the developing economies need to unite and raise their voice collectively. They need to speak about the unfair treatment meted out to them. A step in this regard has been taken by countries like India and China in important forums like UN and WTO. These breakout countries can act like role models and help create a more equitable world.

Another country is India, developing country , it may choose to manufacture and sell cheap products to any overeas countries to earn high GDP trade income. Till about 1750s, India was one of the largest economies in the world, contributing close to 25% of the world GDP. It was called the 'Golden Bird' and its products were world famed. The country has had huge trade surpluses for centuries through export of spices, finished cloth ('light woven air', it was called), and diamonds; all exotic products to that time period. It also had a thriving shipbuilding industry. There were accounts of Roman Establishments worrying about their riches syphoning off to India, because of the love of their woman towards Indian Cloth. India, thus essentially provided what the world desired & craved for, taking very few in return. This is despite the fact that it had one of the largest populations of that time. Then how come Indians achieve that richness and advancement, which seems difficult now? It is because, India was a hotbed of skilled people, who created exotic products, which were taken to the world by merchants in Indian built ships, which in turn were financed adequately by an established network of local people. So, although, India is not one high technologic development country, but it can choose what kinds of general cheap products to manufacture or catch any natural resources, e.g. growing up fishing industry, diamond industry. It is any one developed countries can not own strengths to compete to India easily.

Modern India and the ilk, are that they should spend more on Education and encourage Individual/SMEs (Small and Medium scale Enterprises), through adequate financing. The educational infrastructure should go to every nook and corner of the country like the 'temple complexes' providing accessible and affordable education, in the form of 'community colleges' in the US & 'skill enhancement centres'. Governments should support with adequate funds to create world-class universities of yesterday like 'The Nalanda', to provide cross-functional education and focus on innovation. The population should be encouraged to innovate & produce products, the world desires, like the 'light muslin cloth' or the 'iPhone' of the modern day, which shall bring huge trade surpluses. Industrialization should be decentralized through support for SMEs rather than purely going for High scale Industries. The financial infrastructure should be expanded enough to provide the financial support to every citizen, through banking services. Thus, on the whole, history can provide us with a lot of lessons on how to go about things, provided we have the interest to see from where we have come from. These lessons can be modified and applied to the current times, for we know these lands have done it before, for centuries. But, the only thing that requires here is 'Conviction' and if every country starts working on building these capacities, they becoming developed economies is just a matter of time!

● Climate change will impact developed countries to continue develop

Why does climate change impact developed countries to continue develop more easily? It is one natural environment hurt problem , due to human,e.g. businessmen their damage our global natural environment behaviors, to cause any one developed countries may become developing countries in future one day in possible. I shal indicate the reasons as below:

The effects of climate change will not be uniformly distributed across the globe and there are likely to be winners and losers as the planet warms. Applying a broad brush to climate effects, developing countries are more likely to disproportionately experience the negative effects of global warming. Not only do many developing countries have naturally warmer climates than those in the developed world, they also rely more heavily on climate sensitive sectors such as agriculture, forestry and tourism. As temperatures rise further, regions such as Africa will face declining crop yields and will struggle to produce sufficient food for domestic consumption, whilst their major exports will likely fall in volume. This effect will be made worse for these regions if developed countries are able to offset the fall in agricultural output with new sources, potentially from their own domestic economies as their land becomes more suitable for growing crops. Moreover, developing countries may also be less likely to create drought resistant harvests given the lack of research funding.

Wild weather weighs on economies

The increased frequency and severity of extreme weather will weigh on government budgets. The aftermath of natural disasters often falls on authorities who are forced to spend vast amounts on clear-up operations and healthcare costs that come with experiencing extreme weather. Revenue reductions may also be experienced by countries heavily dependent on tourism or on selling fishing rights, fo

The effects on negative environment influence to developed countries and developing countries

As developed countries face an increasing strain on domestic budgets, fewer resources in the form of aid and economic development funds will flow to developing countries. The governments of these nations will be forced to channel resources away from productive and growth-enhancing projects towards countering the costs of extreme weather. Such effects will damage near-term growth prospects. Furthermore, developing countries are likely to have less capacity to rebuild. The time required to recover from natural disasters will be prolonged and if longer than the frequency in which such disasters occur, many developing economies could remain in a constant state of reconstruction.

Africa and Asia most at risk

Highly vulnerable regions in the emerging world include Sub-Saharan Africa and South and South East Asia, according to the World Bank. In South Asia, cities such as Kolkata and Mumbai will face increased flooding, warming temperatures and intense cyclones. Loss of snow melt from the Himalayas will also reduce the flow of water into the Indus Ganges and Brahmaputra basins. Meanwhile in South East Asia, Vietnam's Mekong Delta, which produces most of the rice, is especially vulnerable to rising sea levels. For Sub-Saharan Africa, food security will be a major challenge due to droughts and shifts in rainfall. Many developing nations are situated in low latitude countries and it is estimated that 80% of the damage from climate change may be concentrated. Consequently, higher agricultural yields, lower heating requirements and lower winter mortality rates are a handful of economic benefits climate change may bring, although these benefits may diminish as warming continues.

However, the prediction that developing countries will be disproportionately affected is reinforced by Standard and Poor's research on the influence climate change will have on sovereign risk. Recognising that climate change is a global mega-trend impacting sovereign risk through economic, fiscal and external performance, they find that lower-rated sovereigns appear most exposed. Based on these measures we can interpret the results in part as the susceptibility of an economy to climate change.

How poor climate change influences UK developed growth
In the UK, the average temperature is now 1°C higher that it was 100 years ago and 0.5°C higher than it was in the 1970s. As a higher latitude country, it is believed that the UK will fare better than many developing nations as global warming progresses. That is not to say the nation will escape the costs of climate change - particularly given its significant coastline where rising sea levels pose an obvious threat. According to scientists estimate of the cost of floods to the UK economy as a result of 3°C - 4°C of warming are in the region of 0.2% - 0.4% of GDP annually by the middle of the century, if flood management efforts are not strengthened.

In England, the south and parts of Yorkshire and Humberside are forecast to experience the greatest impact from flooding by 2050 . Aside from increased flooding, water availability will become progressively more constrained and droughts more frequent .Milder winters and the associated decline in cold-related mortality rates will be countered by a greater prevalence and severity of heat waves, bringing with it a higher number of heat-related mortalities. Finally, with the agricultural sector contributing approximately just 0.6% of GDP, the benefits of longer growing seasons will be marginal to the economy.

In conclusion, climate change may also indirectly affect the UK economy through global supply chains. The UK may both export to and import from climate-sensitive countries. The subsequent influence of climate change in these economies may feed through to the domestic economy through lower demand for exports or higher prices of imports.

CHAPTER FOUR

# FACTORS INFLUENCE HUMAN FUTURE HIGH TECHNOLOGICAL DEVELOPMENT FAILURE

Why do developed countries need to improve on culture, education, medical technologyl development aspects?

I shall attempt to explain that why America, Japan, England and India these four countries ought need to improve on above sevearal aspects as below:

Firstly, I shall explain that why Japan still needs to improve itself country technology development, although Japan had been a technological mature development country in long time. In Japan technological development history, Japan had owned high technological development on technological products manufacture aspect, such as electronic rice cookers, artificial intelligent rice cookers cars, televisions etcl technological products. But when

Germany had also began to develop high technological products in global technological prodict market. In basic, all any similar Japan technological products. Germany had also owned high technological skills to manufacture to sell in global high technological products marekt.

So, nowadays, Germany may still be Japan's high technological product main competitor. It means that global homeholders technology products consumers, car buyers must choose any Germany and Japan high technological products to compare which are better quality in order to satisfy their useful need.s Hence, in global high technological products market, Japan won't be still high technological product leader as past history. If Japan did not continue to improve its technology, Germany will be the future high technology product leader to replace Japan, hence Japan can not neglect to consider how to continue to improve its technology development.

IN the past, science and technology in Japan is focused in vehicle manufacture technology, consumer electronic, robotics, medical devices, space exploration and film industry. For example, Japan's focus on intensive mathematics education and the reverence for engineers in Japanese culture aids enginnering talent development which as produced advances in automative engines, television display technology, videogames , optical clocks etc. On aerospace exploration aspect Japan had conducted space and planetary research., aviation research and development of space and satellites. On nuclear power development technology, since 1973, Japan has been looking to become less dependent on imported fuel and start on depend on nuclear energy. On electronic development aspect, Japan is well known for its electronic industry throughout the world, and Japanese electronic products account ofr a large share in the world market. However, Japan had beed a leading nation in scientific research, particularly biomedical research.

However, all of above technology, Germany will own advance technology to replace Japan to develop its products to sell to global easily. Germany had innovated its technology, e.g. the self -driving cars of the near future depend on precise digital geolocation data to navigate to arrive at destinations. So, Germany's non-manual driving vehicles innovation may be future nay countries car users' suppliers. Also, its battery technology is also one of future high technology mission 2021. Germany government began to support the construction of autonomous capacities in battery cell production to secure technological maximally exploit the battery calue chain. Germany government should continue to support electronic battery cell manufacturers, to drive force in the growing market for electronic cars and the goals of continuing to build their motors in Germany in the future.

Is Germany technology advanced? I believe that it is true, in the index's eighth edition for 2020, Germany was named the most technologically advanced nation, followed by South Korea, and Singapore, Germany is most known for its engineering, different high technological invention etc. aspect. Why is Germany so technologically advanced? Because Germany had been an academic powerhouse for a long time and as such education is focused on technological aspect. It's education goal is for good ideas to be translated quickly into innovative products and services. Moreover, Germany also considers Hyper automation, the distributed cloud, technological development. Some technological leaders predict the future high technological development countries may include: China, South Korea, United States , Singapre , United Kingdom, Russia, Japan and Germany .

The possible number or rank technological development countries rank may be 1 South Korea rank 2 ,ay be United States, rank 3 may be Japan, rank 4 may be Sweden nowadays. However, Germany may be future rank 1 technological leader, because Germany is so good at engineering. Germany's engineers borne out of the country are world leaders in their field, reowned for their dedication to precision, function and power. Over the years, Germany engineers have maintained their reputation to help Germany technology development products to as a top exporter of machinery and industrial equipment.

Moreover, in human development history, Germany are smart, when Germans are the most intelligent people in Europe, the British have an edge over rivals in France when it comes to the grwy matter , a new league of IQ scores has shown. The scored 94 and Germans were tap of the table with an IQ of 107, according to Richard Lynn, who headed the study. However, why is German technology will be the best. The major factor for Germany's success is that it has managed to homegrown scientific research and expertise to move up the technological ladder, concentrating on innovative products and processes not easily copied or undercut by cheap wages. The textile industry is a case in point, hence it causes that future Germany's technology development may be Japan's future one main competitos in technological product development market. So, it is right time, Japan needs to continue to research its new technological invention in order to improve its technological development to be the best to compare other high technological development countries.

Secondly, I shall discuss that why US needs to improve or change itself country's culture to let many different countries people can adopt to live. For example, nowadays, COVID 19 illness is serious to influence any one country people live. IN fact, US ia a developed country, it is global countries only one leader to encourage different countries people to live. Also, US is one comfortable living people to let global immigrants to feel. But, when COVID 19 disease occurred, some US people feel that it is possible due to Chinese people , they contact COVID 19 disease to cause many US people get this kind of disease. However, it is none evidence to prove this kind of illness may be caused by Chiese to cause many US people die. So, US, opening culture began to change worse, e.g. some US people began to hate overseas immigrants to live itself country, it is possible due to many US people feel afraid to contact overseas immigrants, they may bring COVID 19 disease in their bodies, so when US people they contact these overseas COVID 19 disease immigrants, they may get this kind of disease . SO, it seems that US people's opening accept to let overseas immigrant living policy has

changed to prohibit them to immigrate to live US easily.
However, I feel that US 's closing culture mind can not bring its social development to improve more easily. US ought to change its social culture has more opening cultural mind as before how it accepted different countries immigrants to choose US to live. Hence, it brings this question: What challenges US may encounter if it can be change its new cultural mind to accept more overseas immigrants to live easily? The challenges may include: American needs to understand themselves value and learn about what is important to Americans know why Americans value independence, equality and being on time. Americans will need see they are direct and informal and why competition, work ethic, and buying things are important in the US. American probably had strong traditions and culture that they valued. In the UNited States, there are also important American values are the things that are most important to Americans. For example, one of the main American values is independence. Independence is sometimes referred to US individualism. Americans are very proud of being self reliant, or being able to take care of themselves. American children tend to leave the home earlier than in oterh cultures, if they continue to live at home, they might be asked to pay rent or contribute to the house. So, Americans expect anyone who is able to work to do in order to support themselves. Also, Americans value privacy and their own space, when in some cultures wanting privacy may be seen as a bad thing, many Americans like to have alone time and may be private abour certain topic. In conversations, many Americans are private about certain things and do not want to talk about them, such as age, how much money they make, or their political, sexual and religious views. Americans often give each other more space in public situations than people in other cultures . They tend to stand with a bit of space between them, typically the distance of direct. This means that they often tell you what they think and they will be assertive about when they want.
Some peoples of American-style directness,, such as in conversation, if an American disagrees with youropinion, they

might tell you, this does not mean they do not like you, just that they may have a different area. In classes, Americans may challenge their teachers' ideas. IN some culture, it is impolite to disagree with your teacher, it is never is rude to ask for help. Most Americans love to help and need very little encouragement to become good friends and neighbors.

However, I feel that America has lose equality value. Although, many newly immigrants moved to America to follow American team. They believed that if you worked hard, you could move up in society. But, today, more and more people realize the American dream is not true. Many people who work very hard do not have very much money. Often people who love from privileged backgrounds have an easier time moving up in the world. Still, the idea of equality is an important part of US culture.

So, COVID 19 disease occurrence had explained that US began have inequality culture difference causes, discrimination to overseas immigrants, e.g. Chinese. Americans discrimination behavior began to cause. American ought change itself new culture to traditional culture to accept different countires clever immigrants skills, talent people mind in order to help itself country to continue develop more advanced society to be world leader position.

Thirdly, I shall discuess why England needs to improve education. What negative impacts will happen, if UK does not continur improve education as well as its neglect on improvement education, how it will bring negative impact to its studetns minds in society? Why growth is the key to improve UK education development? Conventional wisdom states that smaller schools provide students with a better education . But studies of education systems around the world, show that growing schools could actually solve UK's poor student outcomes.

Nowadays, the UK's school system is in trouble, despite the fact that the last two decades have seen massive changes in the UK's education sector. UK education report indicated that in the past 15 years, the UK's four countries have spent $550 UK billion on operating and enhancing their secondary schools. IN the same period, England alone closed 35% of its schools ( 1,500 institutions) and opened almost 2,000 new ones . Nonetheless, little has improved UK education report indicated that in 2026, only 65% of all English pupils graduated with five or more grade as compared with 50% 15 years ago, at a cost od $37 billion per percentage point of improvement. The US was as a wholw spent the 8 th largest amount of 34 OECD countries, but only came, 19 th in mathemactics, 16 th in reading and 14 th in science.

So, what 's going wrong to cause UK students have worse learning performance. The reasons may include: Neglecting all four nations education reforming. Education in the UK is devolved to the four nations that make up the British union. For this reason, most of qualifications data relates only to England, although total spending figures are mostly UK wide. Academy shcools are amodel of schooling that is available only in England. There is no provision for the model in the other three nations of the UK.

The next reason is failure educational strategy. UK education report also indicated that England's strategy over the past 15 years has been to try to improve its education system by fixing its low lights , less than a third of students graduate with five or more GCE grade , reducing their projected lifetime earnings by $140,000. By putting their schools into " special measures" and offering them up for tender to other schools, it hopes that whole education system would improve. BUt, it has not . THe English have thrown more money at the proble,, spending 84% more on each child's education . Then, they did 15 years ago ( $57,000 rather than $31,000), but although half their schools have improved, the other half have declined, and the overall picture is still the same. So, there are still many UK schools can not get UK government help to improve all school students individual learning effort to be better.

- What would have happened if UK government had spent the last 15 years trying to grow their education system bright lights, rather than brighten , their low lights?

UK education improvement strategy is such that a similar change in strategy helped the charity save the children reduce malutrition by 80% in Vietnam over two years, after decades of getting. Instead of trying to solve the poor learning ability of student learning performing problems in their worst areas, UK educators also need to expand a similar improvement education on strategy shift in order to help transform to UK any schools reforming educational policies in success.

Hence, if England had adopted another long term countrywide educational strategy, where all schools work together to improve standards across the UK in order to access all schoools resources, facilities and entracurricular activities and it could shown that good teachers in both schools can teach anyone. Then, most of UK teachers can know their subject inside out and quickly adapt their teaching methods to different needs. Consequently, when UK can imporve most of UK students learning effort to the best performance, as better educated students are more knowledgeable, money when they can attribute their the best effort to their society in the future. Then, UK society can be developed to reach the most top level, because UK's future development must depend on its next generation's help. If future UK education can train many talent students to attribute to social different aspects, such as technology, medical , business, construction etc. different professional aspects . UK future social development may be improved to be better to compare present society development. So, UK government can not neglect how to improve all UK student individual learning performance in order to help every UK student to pursue their abilities to prepare to attribute to UK future society devleopment successfully.

Finally, I shall discuss why India will need to improve medical technology. Recently, world news reported that INdia has many people are killed by COVID 19 disease. India is the highest population country. I assume that COVID 19 disease causes many Indians die because India has no enough hospitals, clinics to provide good medical quality to serve these COVID 19 disease contact patients. Due to lack of the best medical skillful doctors and nurses. So, many COVID 19 disease patients can not be saved to their lifes, even in India society, many none of COVID 19 disease contact people, when they contact to the COVID 19 disease people, they can not give good drugs to save themselves lifes. SO, it explains why India has many people are killed by COVID 19 disease in short time . SO, it seems that India lacks enough drugs to supply to these COVID 19 disease patients to cause there are many COVID 19 disease patients die in short time.

This COVID 19 diease attracks India matter occurs, it brings these questions: IS short time shortage of drug supply factor or long time shortage of drug supply factor to cause many COVID 19 disease patients die? Can long time poor medical technology factor cause many Indians die? IS COVID 29 disease the main factor causes many Indians die? India has many people are living. So, India must eed to improve its medical technology in order to solve the number increasing of India people future health challenge. One of the most important and highly debated, elements of India society is the quality of healthcare available to patients. The use of technology increases provider capability and patient access when improving the quality of life for some India clients and saving the lives of others. The India technology role can play in improving health of India. It can help in early detection of health problems. It cn also help in data collected from tests instantly monitor, the conditon of the patient, and then relay that information to the doctors and staff of the overall healthcare system.

However, the factors have made improvement in health conditions possible in India , they may include: A downtrend in communicable diseases, a focus on prevention , reduced neonatal mortality rates, tacking antimicrobial resistance, improved nutrition, using digital health and artificial intelligence for social impact, stronger government accountability. A number of industry analysts have observed that increased accessibility of treatment is one of the most tangible ways that technology has changed healthcase. Health IT opens up may more avenues of exploration and research, which allows experts make helathcare more driven and effectve than it has ever been. Hence, future India may apply these new medical technology, e.g. virtual reality, precision medicine, health wearables, artificial organs, 3D printing, wireless brain sensors, robotic surgery, smart inhalers, they are the main treatment option for asthma and if taken correctly, will be effective for 80% of India patients.

Hence, India must need solve medical technology improvement challenge in order to keep many people lifes , in special for the talent youngers, e.g. doctors, scientists, architects, lawyers, accountants , atc. professionals. I believe that India's medical technology can not been improved to raise quality in order to save many COVID 19 disease patents their lifes. So, many of COVID 19 disease patients can not been saved by good quality if medical drugs in short time. So, if INdia does not hope to lose many young talent professionals, it must need to continue improve its medical technology as soon as possible.

● How can our future social development can be improved ?

Nowadays, globalization cooperation or our societies become one society to any countries leaders is needed. I believe that countries competition will be serious, even we shall attack other countries if any one country can not accept " globalization cooperation mind". I mean that it is only globalization cooperation one way choice, then our societies can be improved or will be become better more easily. For China and America two countries example, recently, because COVID 19 disease caused many Western and Asia countries began feel that COVID 19 disease was caused from Chinese. However, they have no evidence to indicate that COVID 19 disease must be caused from China. Although, before the year end of two years, there are some Chinese had ever travelers to US, then US had many people began to get this kind COVID 19 disease to cause many American die, when they did not believe that COVID 19 disease can cause human dies easily. Until to now, global many people had gotten this kind of illness to vause they die, when the health person contacts the owned COIVD 19 disease sick people . Although some people can be saved after they are saved by drug, but many people can not be saved, when they can not been saved by drug, even they still can not saved after they had been gotten drug. Such as US, UK, India, China, Germany , Korea, Japan, France these countries reported that they had many people could not saved to keep their lifes when they could not believe that they can get COVID 19 disease when they contact to the strange people who may owned COVID 19 diesease easily, when they are sitting down to the same table to eat in restaurants or when the COVID 19 disease strange person and the health person are talking together closely.

So, I believe that it is right time to any countries leaders need to act and to cooperate to find the method to avoid COVID 19 disease attacks any people. I mean the globalization cooperation attitude may nee to ourselves countries leaders . Our country leader can not only consider himself/herself country benefit and neglact to consider other countries benefits. If global humans hope that we can still to improve our culture to be peace or improve our space technology artificial intelligent development manufacturing to the advance level rapidly, or improve our medical technology to the best quality or improve our students learning effort or teachers teaching performance to reach the most satisfactory need to our future any one students. It is only global cooperation way to achieve global improved societies aim. If our societies or any one country leader still only consider how to protect himself/herself country businessmen benefits and leader himself/herself benefits, and rich people benefits , but they neglect to consider any one citizen benefits ,e.g. the low education, poor old age people, low income people in societies.Then, unfair and discrimination will be encouraged to occur in any one country society . Consequently when any one country low education , low income , poor old people can not feel comfortable to lieve in themselves countries. They will feel angry to complain themselves countries governments and leader individual ambitious behavior to influence these group people feel unhappy to live long time in themselves countries.

Consequently, the country's social education level will only continue to worse, even economy will continue recession, as ell as and kind of technologies won't continue improve. Due to our future any one country leader can not keep globalization cooperation mind or positive opening attitude to let any one itself country citizen feels comfortable to live forever. Then, the developed country ,e g. US, UK will not still keep technology development leading position easily. It is possible due to they only consider themselves social benefits, during this COVID 19 disease had been attacking themselves countries. So, they ought also consider other countries , they are attacked by COVID 19 disease, hoe to avoid COVID 19 disease will continue to attack any one country easily.

Hence, we only cooperate to help ourselves to find the best long time method to fight COVID 19 disease . When our countries leaders can cooperate to spend time to sit down to discuss how to fight COVID 19 disease , then I believe that our global societies may been improved more better rapidly as soon as possible in this year.

- Methods to avoid future human developmend failure

Finally, I shall conclude that how we can avoid human development failure. we need to know that human is facing threat of self-benefit behavior. We can follow our development to analyze why we shall encounter failure of improvement stage in our soon future. In our past thousand years, human had developed in success from fishing, agriculture stage till to manufacture industry innovation stage, till to nowadays high technological development stage ,even our future artificial intelligent high technology ( non-manual control machine stage). Although all of our past development , till to nowadays development, it seems that we can develop in success in any technological aspects ,e.g. space, computer , internet , ecommerce , medical technology etc. even future non-manual control (AI) artificial intelligent technology. But, some ways may help us to continue high technological development in success, even damage our future continue high technological development. They may include unfriend or poor culture development, lacking globalization cooperation, self -beefit mind factors.

All of above factors are any countries leades self-benefit mind or negative attitude ( human behavior) to influence our future high technology continue development can succeed in possible. The reason is because that if any one country leader only considers how to protect himself/herself country technological development beefit, it means that he/she does not allow his/her country talent scientists can discess their any new technological invention opinions to let other countries talent scientists to learn ho to improve themselves new technological invention together. This point is the main bad factor to cause human future any kinds of high technological development to delay in possible, because our any kinds of high technological development success, we must depend on global scientists can have chance to share their any kinds of new technological experiments to let they can learn why the scientist can develop the kind of product in success, or why the scientist can not develop the kind of product in success. Then, any one country scientists can absorb other countries scientists their successful or failure scientific experiements in order to improve their any kinds of new technological expeiment to achieve the most satisfactory scientific experiement demand to bring benefit to us. So, globalization cooperation is the only way to avoid human development failure absolutely.

- Why do developed countries need to continue to learn how to improve new technology ?

In fact, there are different between developing and developed countries. Developing countries, such as Afria, Korea, China, Taiwan, these countries are developing, so their IT information , medical, manufacturing technology, artificial intelligence etc. different industries are not mature, they must need to continue improvement to develop their skills in order to satisfy consumers market need. Because social need had been often changing, so these developing countries scientists, businessmen need to have good learning mind to prepare to learn how technological , medical , artificial intelligent, IT knowledge in order to satisfy consumer individual new product useful need and keep market competitive effort in themselves home an overseas consumption markets both more easilu. But, why do developed countries also need to continue to learn how to improve new technology? What negative impacts will bring to developed countries their scientists and businessmen do not continue to improve their new products development or continue to research how to improve their old products to achieve the best quality to order consumers needs.

Nowadays, global consumption market competition is serious. Consumer individual need or demand is increasing, when one consumer feels the kind of old product can not satisfy his/her actual need, he/she will seek to find which brands of products, they have similar function or useful characteristics in order to make comparison to other similar kinds of products. Then, he/she will make final purchase decision. So, when the consumer had habit to use the brand of product, it does not mean that he/she will continue to use this brand of product. He/she may be influenced to change to choose the another brand of similar function characteristics of new product to buy use in this rapid changing competitive market.

Hence, if the developed country's culture is changed to closing mind from opening mind. These developed country, such as US people can not accept to other countries people new, useful, attributing innovativ mind of ideas easily. They only consider or recognite that themselves ideas are the best or the most useful. Consequently, due to their foolish closing minds, their traditional protection themselves believes will cause difficult to continue to improve or develop, because it is possible that there are any other developed countries, e.g. UK, Germany, Japan, they have some talent people, scientists their technological skills may be proficient or more advanced to compare US, itself countries some scientists.

So, I recommend that any developed countries can not only consider to appreciate themselves countries scientists must be the most smart to compare other developed countries. Any one developed country scientists ought need to cooperate with other developed countries scientists to discuss or research any new invention together in order to help themselves technology can been improved rapidly in order invent many different kinds of new products to satisfy consumers themselves often changing useful needs in this global consumption market nowadays.

This developed country Japn is one good example to explain that why its scientists ought need to continue to improve their different technology or science skills as well as learn any new kinds of technology or science knowledge from other developed countries scientists , such as US, UK, Germany together. Because it is only one effective technology and science improvement method ( way) to Japan scientists,when they can accept the other developed scientists different new or innovated opinions as well as they can spend some time to sit down to discuss and cooperate to help themselves old products how to change or innovate new products in order to attract global consumers purchase choice. So, although, Japan had been one developed country long time, its technology development had searched mature stage in the past, But, it can not reprsent that its technology must be more advanced to compare other developed countries, such as UK, US, Germany. Because these any one developed country, their scientists still continue carry on researching how to improve themselves old products to be new. So, it seems that Japan's any old technological products, e.g. smart phones, television, washing machines, rice coolers, products won't bring more attract to persuade global consumers choices. Because US, UK, Germany etc. different developed countries scientists had began to research how to continue improve its traditional old technological products to be more attraction in order to adopt global technological products users needs. For example, developing country India, due to its medical technology is poot, if it hopes to improve itself country technology, it must need to attempt to concentrate on spending money, medical teaching resources on medical technology aspect. India's medical technology improvement must be any kinds of technologies , the most need to improve to compare IT technology, manufacturing technology, artificial intelligent technology, space technology etc. The reason is that India is the highest population country, if its medical technology's cost, it will cause many young talent people die, such as COVID 19 disease occurs to India recently. It causes many Young talent Indians die, due to it lasks enough good medical technology to supply drugs to save them. So, if India government hopes that it can have many talent high skillful technology youngers to serve itself country. It will need to consider how to improve its medical technology in order to fight any possible new kind of illness attack, instead of COVID 19 disease, when India can improve its medical technology to save many young talent scientists' lifes . Then, it won't lose many talent scientists and they can continue to attribute themselves scientific knowledge for India itself country lont time technological science development.

Hence, UK and US both governments need to consider how to allocate enough land to supply to any manufacturing and business operations efficiently, how to help any educational organizations to train talent employees and school organizations to teach talent students, how to supply enough loan to assist any business founders to develop their new businesses in success or create new entrepreneurship. All of these can bring advantages to satisfy their societies needs.

Economists generally agree that highly economic development and growth are influenced by four factors: Human resources, physical capital, natural resource and technology. So, in general, US an UK countries hope they can become highly developed countries have government that focus on these areas. They mean that factors may influence one developed country to continue to become highly developed country, factors may include: accumulation of capital stock, increases in talent labor inputs, such as workers or hour worked, technological advancement. All of these factors may assist UK , US continue to bring highly development benefit. So, UK, US are such as industrialization in developed countries, they need to improve these industrial productivity in order to continue to keep, highly developed countries in possible, these factors may include: long term technological development, improvement quality of human resources, encough availability of finace, efficient managerial talent, efficient government policy and surplus of enough supply of natural factor, e.g. good climate for agriculture, enough natural coal , land natural resource supply. However, they also need to consider these are negative factors to affect them to continue develop, e.g. lack of drive of social motivation for improvement, unproductive social functions, such as war or having very large family sizes, negative social cultures, such as gambling and drinking wine, and lack of skills due to poor training and education . They may be poor social negative factors to influence they continue develop in success.

CHAPTER FIVE

# ORGANIZATION TANGIBLE AND INTANGIBLE RESOURCES FUNCTION

Any organizations must have tangible and intangible resources. Tangible resources may include: Staffs, lands, equipment, producing machines, factory etc. They may help organizations to produce products or provide services to earn profit, e.g. one shop may be the firm's tangible assets if it can be designed to be the best and provide soft music to let customers to listen and provide clourful light design , they may influence they to bring happy consumption emotion in order to attract many customers to stay long time in the shop and increases shopping chance, the salespeople ( staffs ) to attract more customers , they may be influenced to feel enjoy to stay long long time by their services. Although, any customers visit any shops , it must not represent that they quarantee to buy any things before they leave the shop. However, I beleive that any business , their products functions and prices is one influential factor to persuade consumers to do shopping activities, their shop design attraction feeling may be also another main factor to persuade them to do shopping decision because when the consumer feels the shop is comfortable , it will cause he/she feels enjoyable to stay long time in the shop. Consequently, shop design attraction may be another influential intangible resource factor to encourage consumers to buy any things easily, if they can be influenced to stay long time in the shop by the ship design attraction. It is one kind of feeling factor to excite consumers to do shopping decision. SO, shop may be one important organization fixed asset resource to influence consumer individual purchase desire in any business environment. It is one good exmaple organizational tangible fixed asset redsource to help any organizations to create income.

The another kind of intangible resources, they are not seen by any customers and they can not be toughed by any customers. BUt they are organizational resources, they also may help any organizations to earn income. Why can intangible resource help organizations to earn income? I shall explain as below:

Customer services and staff skills, they may be organiztional intangible resources and they may help any organizations to create income. For example, when one shop has one kindly and friendly salespeople, when any one customer enters this shop, he will say" Good morning", " Good afternoon", "Good night" and when the customer leaves this shop, he will say " Goodby". Even, when the customer has not bought any thing till to leave this shop, this salesperson also speaks " Goodby". So, all of shop visitors, when the salesperson sees them, he must speaks above words, so any one must feel he is polite person and he can represents this shop's polite image also. Although, some shop visitors do not buy anything when they are staying in this shop, but they must feel that this salesperson's attitude is polite to let them to feel. THis salesperson can bring happy feeling to let all shop visitors feel. So, he must not be complainted easily, because when this salesperson discovers any one person is staying to close to any one producg shelf location in the shop, he will walk to the person to enquire him" DO you need I help you?" politely. Although, it is possible that this person won't need this salesperson to help him, but this salesperson can let this shop visitor to feel that he does not need find any one salesperson to enquire when he feels that he needs purchase help, e.g. whether the shirt has small size stock, or the shoe has organge colour etc. product information enquiries. SO, this salesperson can let this shop visitor feels he can take care to his purchase choice behavior and he can do and purchase help in this shop any time. So, this salesperson , his excellent service performance can let any one shop visitor feels service satisfaction, instead of his essential sale customer service performance. IN fact, this salesperson may let many shop visitors to feel that he does not only considerate whether whom is his real customer in order to enquire any purchase help. The non purchase plan shop visitors may also feel his kindly customer service help during they are staying in shop any time. So, this salesperson's polite and kindly customer service attitude may influence many non purchase planning shop visitors feel happy to see him in this shop. Consequently, it explains why salespeople excellent customer service performance which may help any businesses to increase customers number. It may be one kind of intangible organization resource to any organizations. I mean that when the shop can train many salespeople to raise customer service sale performance improvement.

Overall, these excellent customer service salespeople mus thelp this business to increase customer number easily, because this shop's all salespeople thier positive emotion may influence any one shop visitor feels enjoyment when they can feel they are taking care to their purchase choice need when they are staying in this shop any time. So, the minute, that the shop visitor does not plan to choose to buy any kinds of products, it does not represent that he does not plan to choose to buy any kinds of products next minute. So, any salespeople their excellent customer service performance may influence any one shop visitor to do purchase planning decision any minute. It seems that " salespeople customer service performance feeling" may be one kind of long time intangible resource to help any businesses to earn income in possible. Hence, it explains that any organizations must have tangible and intangible organizational resources to assist them to develop their businesses in long time success. They are essential elelments to influence whether the business's customers number can increase or decrease.

For computer sale business example, its tangible resource may be computer shop and intangible resource may be computer salespeople skills, because if any visitors feel this computer shop's computer desktop or laptop products can be putted in the right and easy seeking locations on any shelves, e.g. the low range price of laptops or desktops are putted on the lowest shelf position as well as the high range price of laptops or desktops are putted on the highest shelf position. So, when the planning purchase of desktop or laptop shop visitors may compare the different design of laptops or desktops their low range price or their high and low shelves locations easily. So, laptops and desktops putting on shelves position, they may influence any one desktop or laptop buyer individual final purchase choice decision. If the laptop planning purchase visitor, he plans to buy one low price of laptop, when he discovers there are all low range price of laptops are putting on the shelf loe position. Then , he may feel convenience to choose any one kind of low price of laptop design products from the lowest range shelf location easily. So, computer shops' computer putting shelves positions may be one kind tangible resource factor to influence any one computer buyer to choose any one kind of design of laptop or desktop priduct convenience. Their computer product choice time whether it is long or short may influence their final computer purchase decision. Hence, the shop's computers ' putting on shelves positions may be one essential tangible resources to influence any one computer visitor to do purchase decision.

The computer shop salespeople computer knowledge may be another intangible factor to influence any one computer buyer decision. For example, when one planning laptop purchaser wants to know whether the laptop's any function, if he enquiries to the computer salesperson, he ften let him to feel that his explanation can not satisfy his any enquiries about the design of laptop product function knowledge, e.g. how to set up password for this computer privacy. If the computer salesperson lets the planning computer buyer to feel that he is difficult to teach him how to set up the passwrod for the computer to use. Then, the computer salesperson's innocence of computer password set up knowledge which may influence the planning computer buyers makes final non purchase decision to this computer, because his innocence can let him to feel this computer is difficult to set up password , if he is one foolish computer user.

Hence, this computer shop's all computer salespeople their computer knowledge, they may influence any one computer buyer final purchase decision. They must need to be trained to learn how to use any one new design of desktop or latop computer products before they are employed to be salespeople in this computer shop。SO, their computer knowledge may be this computer shop's intangible resource to influence this computer shop's customers number to increase or decrease every day. Hence, decision on any organizational tangible and intangible resources to the organization, they depend on whether what kind of the business needs to sell what kinds of products.

The organization is where resources come together . Organizations use different resources to accompolish goals, e.g. human resources, financial resources, physical resources, and
information resources. SO, managers are responsible for managing the resources to accomplish goals. Organizational resources are all assets that are available to a firm for use during
the production process. The four basic types of organizational resources are human, monetary, raw material and capital. Managing organizational resources is the ability to understand and effectively manage organizational resources ( e.e. people, materials assets , budget). This is demonstrated through measurement, planning and control of resources to maximize resources.

Company resources include tangible assets , such as its plant, equipment, finances, and location, human assets , in terms of the number of empllyees, their skills and motivation and intangible assets ( such as technology, patents and copyrights, culture and reputation).

It brings this question: What makes organizational resource unique, in resource based view? Resources are available when they allow a firm to take advantage of opportunities or threats in its external environment. Many resources can either be immitated or substituted over time to any organizations. Hence, effectively managing resources helps companies more consistently deliver projects and services on time. This is because better resource management helps to improve insight into resources availability as well as improves timeline projections. Hence, the types of resources in management they may include: Human resource, natural resource, project resource, financial management, facility management, entertrise asset, public asset management.
ON conclusion, I believe that a company's most important resources may be human captial, such as talent employees, their technical knowledge may be intangible resource asset to help the organization to develop its business in longf term success.

Internet will be intangible technology knowledge resource to e-commerce organization
New economy brings new way of resource management. The old loyalty and job security -based organization changes, organizations know that the assets are largely made up employees ( HRM), but many new organizations begin to believe technology is important assets, such as Amazon is global ecommerce delivery service organization. It seems internet high technology is its important intangible resource to help it earn global e-buyers number increases . So , many organizations began to believe that technology will be important resource, such as internet can provide online business chance. With all the businesses are taking full advantage of internet, for example, the US department estimates that the value of retail e-commerce in 2000 year was about $25 billion, which represents less than 1% of US retail sales. Despite this, interest in e-business

remains high.

- Why internet may be main technology resource to organizations?

E-commere needs strategy in order to win competitors, questions include: What criteria do customers use to choose between our firms and competitors? How do the best employees decision whether to join? What business environment attracts and keeps the best suppliers making with our firms? What characteristics draw the most royal invesdtors to our firms? e.g. Amazon . com's web site and Wal-mart's can apply internet technology resource to create each e-store to let e-buyers to choose any kinds of products to buy athome conveniently. Hence, internet technology, even future other kinds of new technology may be main technology resources to organizations, when they can help organizations to raise sale competitive effort.

I mean that digital economy will be one kind new digital resource to future any organizations. The essential piece is the knowledge, it is what give it life and what makes it an interesting and fulifulling purchase and sale channel for people to spend their time , such as e-commerce virtual organization may be leaded to let purchase and ale transactions carry on easily from online websites. Hence, internet may be main knowledge management ( intellectual capital) resource to any e-commerce organizations. It is about the storage, transfer knowledge.

For Amazon publish example, e-books will be knowledge as an object, like a book in library. Amazon can apply internet technology to help it to sell any author's ebooks from its book estores. So, ebooks are Amazon's knowledge resources to help it to create readers incomes. E-books is intangible knowledge resource to Amazon . Any authors' paper and ebooks will be sold cheap price to help Amazon to attract global readers to choose to buy its ebooks from its different countries e-webstores at home conveniently.

Hence, any e-commerce organizations also need HRM ( emanagers ) to help them to deliver a superior value ( world class capabilities) in both te virtual and physical world. E-management will be another main human resources to e-commerce organizations. Why does e-management will be future main HRM resource to e-commerce organization? The reasons may include:

E-management demands in sort of managerial/e-commerce sale strategy effort, skills at positioning the firm within a networm of industries, e-management also demands the ability to see how the firm fits into a value creation-e-management is different because doing it work requires the e-engineering of business eco-systems, e-management demands the ability to be connected to thousands of inputs about specific changes among many industry participants , such as suppliers , customers, employees, competitors, media and shareholders.

Effective e-management requires the ability to monitor developments that can change with unusually high frequency. However, it is also essential that e-managers distinguish between the few meaningful inputs and the many inputs that have limited significance, ability to sustain organizational change, effectie e-managers monitor changes in their markets. So, instead of e-commerce organizations need to employ talent e-managment staffs to help them to manage overall e-commerce organizations. E-leading staffs ( HRM) is another main HRM need. E-leaders need to know how to design online brochures, e.g. online brochures simply involved putting a company's market materials on the web. in order to attract or persuade online buyers visit its websites and choose the most right price of product to buy easily. E-leaders need to lead front-office transactions which involved putting customer facing customers , such as placing on order on the web when leaving back-office activities, such as order fulfillment unchanged.

E-leaders also need to integrate online online purchase transactions in which a firm actually linked its front -office and back -office systems and processes in a fashion, e.g. most companies have developed online brochures , in order to let online advertisement tool to attract e-buyer individual purchase choice from its webstores. Hence, future any e-commerce organizations must need (HRM ( e-leaders and e-managers) to help them to bring innovation in order to achieve maximize profit aim. So, internet webstores, e-leaders , e-managers may be future e-commerce organization main resources. So, e-commerce organizations, manages are actors at three levels: In the front line , as entrepreneurs, in the middle , as facilitators, and integrators, at the top as institution builders.

Hence, future new economical society, it creates e-commerce organizations number increases, when consumers began to accept online purchase transaction activities. Hence, it causes e-commerce began to feel internet ( e-webstores, e-leaders, e-managers), they will be the most influential resources ( intangible knowledge managment and tangible URM both resourcees to influence their success or failure.

- Why doe e-commerce organization believe ( e-webstore design, e-leaders and e-managers) will be main organizational resources?

The most important question: It asks when e-buyers visit their webstores, wo are their target customers and shich needs of theirs are their trying to satisfy? For exap,e many airlines , e.g. American airlines, China airlines began to feel online e-tickets sale channel is more easily than paper ticket shop sale channel, because many air passengers began to accept e-ticket/online ticket purchase choice more than visiting airline shops . They feel that they do not want to waste time to visit airline shops. They like to pre-book to buy e-ticket to pay from the airline e-websote conveniently. Hence, e-webstore design knowledge management , e-leaders and e-management webstore management skill will be future any one e-commerce organizations their main tangible and intangible resources ( assets ) to help their e-commerce businesses development.

On conclusion, I believe that the current economy is not a high-tech economy or an internet economy, not an m-commerce economy , but instead customer econoomy. Customers need to gather with information and access, they are demanding, fair, global price, they are demanding that compares deal with them using the distribution channel , they choose manufacturing direct and through dealers and retailers. Base on those factors, they encourage future many e-commerce organizations cause organization change traditional resouce concept, such as land, capital equipment, tangible resource began to change to e-commerce organization's intangibel and tangible resource, such as knowledge management to e-online web store design skills, e-leaders and e-managers e-stores sale management strategy and e-buyer product research and brochure online advertisement design skill. All of these knowledge management skill will be future organizations' main resources to help them to create new economic competition effort.

Organization resources defination

What are organizational resources ? What do organizational resources mean? What kinds of organizational resources are needed? What negative impact may be influenced if organizations lack enough resources to influence organizational development? Does working time belong to organizational time resources to influence employee individual efficiency e.g. how arranging enough employee to do the identified task in the most short time in order to achieve the most efficient performane? I shall attempt to identify examples to explain above questions as below:

In general, organizational resources are all assets, that are available to a firm for use during the production process. The four basic types of organizational resources are human, monetary , raw materials and capital. Organizational resources are combined, used and transofrmed to finished products during the production process. For organizational human resource example, human resource activities full under the following five core functions: staffing, development, compensation, safety and health core functions.

● HR resource

HR conducts a wide variety of activities. However, in any organizations, the major resources used by organizations are often described as follow ( 1) human resources (2) financial respirces (3) physical resources and (4) information resources. Managers are responsible for acquring and managing the resources to accomplosh goals. Hence, in organizational HR aspect, it may include these function, such as retirement and selection, performance management , learning and development, succession planning, compensation and benefits, human resource information systems. Because considering that for many organizations employees themselves represent a significant cost to the business, if the organization can use its employees in efficiency.

Then, it can avoid human resource in excess or in surplus on wasting challenge. Then , its employee cost or salary can be reduced. I t means that it does not need to employ in excess employees number, but the organization can still achieve itself the most efficient performance. Hence, any organizations must need to learn how to avoid " in excess employees number supply or wasting employee working behaviors" challenge . Because if some tasks do not need many employees to work together, it can still be achieved efficiency . Then , the organization ought not employee too many or excess employees to finish the kind of task. Thus, learning how to use efficient human resources, it can help organizations to avoid wasting working time to any departments employees. For example, when one factory has limited land to be supplied to become warehouse in order to help it to keep sticks. If it has excess logistic or factory workers number. Then, they are wasting working time to do not important tasks in warehouse, it means that if the factory has only one warehouse, but its area is small, it can allow maximum 50 workers to stay in the warehouse , but the warehouse has above 100 workers are staying to deliver goods in the small warehouse . Then, they must not actieve the most efficiency , even their delivery or transport goods performance will be influenced to worse by noise and crowd warehouse working environment. Hence, excess employees number in any working environment, which can not improve organizational performance or riase efficiency any organizations can not neglect " excess employees number" organizatinal HR resource arranging issue.

The solution concerns arranging the most right or the most exact empllyees number in order to supply to any organizational departments. Then, the organization can avoid wasting employee individual talent, reducing employing cost, improvig performance, achieving the most efficiency. Resource capacity means resource pool who are available in the organization to take up to appropriate human resource arrangement to assist any departmental development in long term efficiency. Hence, organizational human rsources may become talent tangible assets or foolish tangible assets. It depends on how the organization's resource capacity tasks arrangement to every employee in different departments. If the organization neglects how to arrange every employee task in the most exact or the most appropriate employees number in the department.

The department's efficiency must be caused worse, because excess employees number, it can not help it to achieve the most efficiency aim, even it may influence the excess employees , themselves feel waste working hours to do the not essential or not important tasks. Then, the organization may cause talent employee to become foolish employee. Otherwise, the organization's efficiency to be worse, because when the department has not enough employees to work. Then , any one employee may feel hard to work, his/her emotion may be influenced to negative, then his/her workig behavior may b inefficiency or lazy working. On consequence, the organization may bring economic loss, due to employee individual lasy working behavior, negative working emotion, even high working pressure may be caused, when one employee needs to do more , then the employee's task, but his/her salary can not increase. He/she will feel unfair to compare the another department employee, he /she does not need to spend long working hours or overtime to work per day. SO, any organization needs to avoid shortage employee supply or excess employee supply issue to any departments. Appropriare employees number is the best strategy in order to raise overall organizational efficiency.

● Time resource

Instead of human resource, land, raw material, earth natural resource, electricity, gas may be organization resources . Whether time may be organizational resources, organizational time management vires time as a scarce resource that must be invested as effectivity. Time is an infinite resource . If not properly managed on in an organization. It can have a negative impact on both employer's and employee's productivity. So, organizations should ensure that workers are well equipped to manage time in their duties.So, in management view, any organization managers must need to consider how to manage time, eg . how to arrange employees to work in different departments in order to achieve the most efficiency. They need to understand which resources are in short supply and focus on the prioritizing work across shared resources, they need agree on a common approach, they also need to realize resource management is an ongoing process. Thus, time is an often ignored but invaluable resource in any organization. All activities be it procurement.

An organization's time, in contrast, goes largely unmanaged. Although, phone calls, email, instant messages , meetings, they are general daily tasks to any organizations managers, but mangers need to know how to arrange the most urgent tasks in prior. For example, if the manager can not arrange a meeting to the discuss client tomorroe, as well as the manager needs to spend two hours to meeting with overall 200 employees to discuss how to solve improving efficiency challenge tomorroe. So, this manager needs to make choice whether he ought spend two hours meeting to the business client, or two hours meeting to 200 employees. If he chooses to meet the business client tomorrow, he will help his firm to win the important business chance, but he can not discuss how to improve efficiency in order to find the best method to let 200 employees to know tomorrow. Thus, tomorrow time management will be one importat time resource to the manager. The manager needs to arrange tomorrow two hours time how to plan business meting or efficiency imporvement meerting either to his 200 employees or the one business client. Because if the manager decided to meet the client, he must need to spend today time to aplan or organize how to arrange either business proposal content for the business client or organizational operational challenge questions and solutions for his 200 employees . So, today time management is also important time resource to influence tomorrow either the success business meeting or the organizational 200 employees meeting. So, it seems that time management may be one important resource to any managers more than general employees in any organizations.

If the manager can know how to manager his/her time to do any prior tasks, then he/she may help the organization to raise efficiency or improve performance. Otherwise, if the manager can not know how arrange what prior urgent task needs to be finished. Then, worse performance or inefficiency may be influenced to cause. So, if the organization manager can know how to make time arrangement, I believe that he can help the organization employees to raise efficiency more easily.

Organization efficient using resources economic method

In behavioral economic view , any organizations can attempt to apply behavioral economy method to use resources efficiently. Organizational excellence framework performance measurement takes a systematic approach . One of the most effective ways of using resources and minimizing that use of work. Calculating task cost in the most efficient economic method to help organizations to reduce cost and avoid resources waste, e.g. using resource management software, technology, planning and taking a systematic approach , which aims to manage the most efficient steps to follow to finish or implement each task in the most shor time as well as avoiding excess employees number.

Organizational resource efficiency means using the organization's limited resources in a sustainable manner when minimising impacts on the organization performance. It allows the organization to create more with less and to deliver greater value with less money. HR, raw material, technology input to carry on any organizational resources efficiently ? Management is the process of using organizational resources to achieve organizational goals of using organizational resources to achieve organizational goals effectively and efficiently through planning , organizing , leading and controlling. An efficient organization makes the most productive use of its resource in the most short time and the most eficiency and the least cost aspects.

- What is efficient use of resources to any organizations in economics?

Economic efficiency implies an economic state in which every resource is optimially allocated to serve each individual or entity in the best way when minimizing waste and inefficiency. whan an economy is economically efficient, any changes made to assist one entity would harm another . Hence, budget how much spending on resources, e.g. employee saley, office and/or plant technological equipment facilities , before making resource expenditure spending decision. Budget is essnetial to help the organization to deduce resource using and excess purchase waste since budget and resource of organizations have interlock or interconnet relationship. If the organization can make exact udget, then it can avoid excess expenditure or waste resource to use. So, organizations need to acquire a talented resource pool , that can lead projects to success, when any kinds of resources are achieved to be supplied to use inn enough . For example, using an effective enterprise resource management system that delivers capabilities. Regardless of the approach and tools used, organizations must determine how to balance to use any kinds of resources efficiently. Thus, in organizational efficient resource using behavioral economy view, the organizational efficiency factor means that influences the efficiency of the organization's use if its resources can be both internal and external, e.g. how implementing strategic plans, they may include selecting what methods and resources to use, and leadning employees on guideline, working in coalitions with organizations around to deliver those needs in the most resource efficient way.

In organizational studies, resource managemetn is the efficient and one resource management technique of resource leveling, of finding the answers to the question, how to use available resource efficiently, effectively and economically ot organization resource expense. SO , resource management is the process of allocating resources and allocating.

● What is meant by economic using of resource to organizations?

Economic resources are the factors used in producing goods or providing services. Economic resources can be divied into human resources, such as labors and management, and non humann resource, such as land, capital , goods, finished resources and technology , for example, natural resource is a key input in the production process that stimulates economic growth. Natural resources have limited direct economic use in satisfying human need, but transforming them into goods and services enhances their economic value to the socirty. So, if the country has many organizations know how to use their natural resources input in that production processes. Then, they can create themselves economic benefits directly and attribute economic benefit to society indirectly.

Thus, the types of economic organizations can be identified, there are subsistence recipreocal exchange with subsistence, peasant with primary reliance on self-produced food, but containing some exhange elements, market-commercial , redistribution or state socialist. Thus organizations need to learn hoe to use themselves organizational resources efficiently. Organizational resources are all assets that are to a firm for use during the production process. The four basic types of organizational resources are human, monetary, raw material and capital. Organizational resources are combined , used and transformed into finished products during the production process. So, a business that understands how to use resources efficiently. resource management is the process of allocating resources in order for a company to grow easily.

Organizational economic is used to study transactions within individual firms and determine management approach to managing resources. It is broken down into thee major subjects: agency theory, transaction cost economic and property rights theory. Agency theory is a priinciple that is used to explain and resolve issues in the relationship between business principles and their agents. Most commonly, that relationship is the one between shareholders as principles, and company executives as agents. Agency theory is used to understand the relationship between agents and principals. The agent represents the principal in a particular business transaction and is expected to represent the best interests of the principal without regard for seld interest. So, when the relationship between shreholders and company executives is kept the best.

Transaction cost economic is understood as alternative modes of organizing transactions ( governance structure, such as markets, firms and bureaus) that mininize transactions costs. This, cost is the primary determinant of such as firm's decision whether it is the most right ( the best) or the worst decision. It will influence the firm ho to spend resource behavior. The cost other than the money price that are incurred in trading good and service. SO, if the organization can often make the best decision to carry on any activites. It will avoid to waste resources efficiently. For example, if transaction cost influces the commission, paid to a stockbroker for completing a share deal and booking fee charges when purchase concert tickets. The cost of travel and time to complete an exhange , it means that transaction cost. So if the organization can make the best or the most reasonable decision to carry on any business activities. Then, its transaction cost can be influenced to reduce the most level in order to bring resources economic benefit. e.g. sunk costs are indpeendent of any event and should not resulting from economic trade in a market.

Property right theory means contracted choice, through ownership, property rights theour clarifies the firm's boundary choice. The maon egal property rights are the right of possession, the righ tof excession. So, for the efficiency of property rights al scarce resources are owned by someone. IN the right property rights approsed to the theory of the firm, I assume that in the case of sale ownership by party-property rights define the theoretical and legal ownership of resources and how resources can be used by organizatin. So, above three major organizational theories can assist organizations to know how to spend resources efficiently.

The relationship between organization resources using and social resources

Resources needers may include societies needers ,e.g. government house material householders , electricity , water , natural resources needers, schools, public houses , land number and area needs etc. as well as business organiztions , office building material, office, plant, land area, number need, equipment facilities limited number . So, when global office and plant business users need to buy more land, equipment materials etc. and electricity , water. Social resources number reduces to bring resourcee shortage challenge causes. Have they have shortage relationship ( resource demand number is more than supply number) between social resources need and business resource need? I shall attempt to explain this question as below:

I assume global business organization number increases, they will need many natural resources, e.g. water, electricity, gas, land to supply for office, plant building , material and staff office electricity, gas, plant , office daily essential power need. So, when global business organizations number increases, they may need to use much raw material and natural resources for equipment facility, office plant building material, even day office, plant electricity , gas power, staff drinking water etc. basic office operational needs, when global business organizations number increase.

The question concerns whether they will cause natural resources shortage to supply to social need , when global business organizatins number increases. First, I shall explains what social resources needers mean as below:

- Social resource are defined as any concrete or symbolic term that can be used as an object of exchange among people ( Foa & Foa, 1980), money, information, goods and services both tangible items , such as are ususally defined the assessment of social need is of central allocation between organization needers and social citizen needers both stakeholders. So, when global human birth rate and life time increases, population number will increase, then their social resources need are also increasing, if global organizaions and population number are increasing in the same time, due to earth natural resources has limit number to supply in order to satisfy organizations and families daily resources need, e.g. building material resources are used to build either to build offices, plants or private houses , public house, lands resources are used either to build private or public houses or offices , plants , water is supplied to either office staffs drinking or families drinking, electricity , gas resources are limited to supply either offices plants use or families private or public houses use. Hence, due to all of earth, but in the same time, global offices , plants, government organizations and families numbers both stakeholders number is continue increasing. They have possible to encounter natural resources shortage issue when natural resources are using much, but they can nt manufacturers to increase by human easily.

● Can responding to resource scarcity help some kinds business grow?

Foe example, the food and agricultural business organizations, e.g. supermarkets, restaurants, they must send plactic material to manufacture plactic bags to supply to supermarket buyers to carry fruits, breads, mil, etc. foods when consumers need to buy the kinds of foods in any supermarkets, if plactic material supply number is decreasing, then a lot plactic bags can not supply to let buyers to carry their foods, due to plactic bags number is shortage , it will cause any supermarket buyers feel inconvenient when they need plactic bags to carry their foods, they choose to buy the kind of foods from supermarket to themselves homes.

So, if plactic bags manufacture material i shortage, it can not be manufactured to plactic bags to supply to global supermarket organizations. Then, the one supermarket can provide enough plactic bags to let them to carry their foods from supermarkets to themselves homes conveniently. The focus on plactic bag resource scareity is not impossible to occur to supermarket organization case. If families are often using plactic bag to carry rubbish daily at home. Then, plactic bags number can not increase to satisfy global supermarkets food plactic bags and families themselves homes rubbish plactic bags both stakeholders need. Plastic bags can not be manufactured to supply to manufacture lot plactic bags supply to satisfy global families rubbish plactic bags home users and supermarkets food plactic bas users needs. Consequently, plactic bags prices may be influenced to increases, when plactic bags demand increases, but supply decreases. It is one good exaple to explain why plactic bag manufacturered material supply decreases, it may influence plactic bags number decreases and price increases, because families home rubbish plactic bags and supermarket food plastic bags need both increase.

Consequence, supermarket cost may be influenced , due to plastic bags number also increase much, if one day shortage of plactic manufacturing material supply number is shortage. So, it seems that food plastis bags using number, they have close relationship to impact supermarket food plastic bags price, if supermarkets lack enough plastic bag number supplies, then they need to increase food price, even the supermarket may lose customers , if it can not supply plastic bags to let them to use the supermarket itself plastic bags to carry fruits, ,ilk, soft drinks conveniently. Hence, plastic bag material may be one kind of important natureal resource for supermarkets, because any one consumer may be influenced to choose another supermarket when he/she feels the another supermarket can supply plastic bags to let him/her to carry on fruits, milks, soft drinks conveniently.

Another kind of natureal resource , such as steel material for restaurants , steel material can help global restaurants to manufacture kniefs, glass sups for restaurants customers to eat food or drink , if much steels are used to manufactured cars product to satisfy car drivers' driving lesiure need , then it may also influence restaurants s' knieves, glass cups price increases, due to cost increase, restaurants need to increase food price to compensate its knief, glass cups price. even, many families feel need to buy many gloass cups to drink water, then it may also influence global glass cups price increase. If one day steel material is shortage , this kind of natural resource must influence restaurants glass cups , knief cost increases. So, their general food price may be influenced to increase. It is not fair to global restaurants food consumers.

Hence, it explains resource shortage may influence some kinds of business cost increases, as well as consumer foods, products services price increases. It means that " resource shortage may influence some kinds of businesses cost increases".

In fact, in our societies, natural resource shortage may influence any kinds of business cost increases, w.g. car manufacturing industry, if one day stell manufacturing material is shortage. it will cause many car manufacturers can not buy enough steels to manufacture cars. When, global car buyers number increases, but global cars number can not increase rapidly, due to steel material can not supply enough. Then, cars prices may be influenced to raise. SO, it seems that steel resource shortage may bring reasonable chance to let global car manufacturers to raise cars prices. When , global car buyes ' new car purchase needs are increasing, hence, natural resource shortage may influence some kinds of business produce prices increase in possible, when the kind of product , such as many people begin to chose to buy new cars, more than second hand cars. The, when steel material supplies shortage, it may influence new car price increases in global can market.It means that any organizations ought not waste natural resource. Otherwise, it may influence their cost increases.

Environmental resource scarcity would likely have been adaptivve in the human evolitionary parst, resources in the environment and organization resource shortage problem might alsoo effect how satisfied they were. Hence, organizations in virtually every industry face the challenge of new managing resources effectively. The influence would run the other way instability as rival, such as big data platforms for e-commerce organizations, e.g. e-book publishers, online sellers. Big data platforms lift limitations on the size of computing resources that can be applied for data, in other words, data storage and e-commerce organizations can significantly influence computing efficiency.

Hence, organizational resources may also influence computer

industry information gathering intangible resources, if the electronic books publish, or online electronic commerce product sellers can gather the most up-date consumer individual purchase behavioral data in short time daily rapidly. Then, they collect the most accurate electronic books readers or the kind of online product buyers past purchase choice in order to judge whther which topics of books are the most popular or which kinds of product to the most popular to let them to implement sale strategy, e.g. whether which topic of e-books prices need to be increased ot decreased, whether which kinds of products prices need to be increases or decreased. So, the big data gathering speed is the technology resource to e-commerce market organizations.

Amazon Organizational Intangible Management Resource strategy

Management accounting science how applies to Amazon ecommerce organization

Management accounting concept can help organizations to do management budget strategies, e.g. margin analysis, capital budget, inventory valuation and product cost budget, trend analysis and forecast . Management accounting also called managerial accounting or cost accounting, is the process of analysis business costs and operations to prepare internal financial report, records and managers decision making process in achieving business goals. However, management accountants depend on standard financial statements containing the earning statement, cash flow statement and balance sheet. In addition , it also makes use of additional finds reports in analysizing the information of the organization including budget performance and cost reports. I shall attempt to explain how management account science can help organizations to analyze cost , why and how changes in order to avoid expense increases or excess cost cases or loss increases.

For Amazon e-commerce publish organization example, Amazon publish is a famous publish organization. It applies internet ( online) channel to help authors to sell electronic books and paper books to different countries readers. It also cooperate to other publishers to deliver any its anthors books to their webstores, so when one reader chooses its publish partner webstores to buy Amazon any author books, then Amazon publish will share royalty income between them. Hence, Amazon publish may be book distribution partner to its other e-publish partners.

- How management accounting cocept can help Amazon publish to manage its cost effectively in order to increase its profit or e-books or paper books sale ability.

Amazon publish is a e-comerce organization. It depends high internet speed to help global authors to register Amazon publish's individual author account , then any global authors may download their book files to produce any ebooks and papers to sell from Amazon publisher webstores as wellas global any readers can apply Amazon publish webstores to buy any author individual paper or ebooks from its web-publish stores rapidly. So, Amazon publish must need have fast speed internet technology to support its books sale ability,

It brings this question: How much does Amazon publish internet expenditure need? Does it need to pay shops rent per month? Because Amazon publish has none any actual book shops to locate in any countries. So, Amazon publish must not pay rent to any countries for its shops. Although Amazon publish does not need to pay rent for any book shops, but Amazon publish needs to pay extra internet expenditure to US internet service provider to support its electronic webstores daily electronic books and paper books every purchase transaction, any countries author individual book electronic files download per day 24 hours . So, Amazon publish must need to pay more expenditure for internet service to support its authors and readers their electronic books and paper books purchase and sale transaction per day 24 hours.

As Amazon publish case, in its financial report indicates , it does not pay any book stores rent expenditure or book stores ( shops) building building expediture on its profit and loss account, but Amazon publish must need to pay internet service expenditure to US internet service provider. Moreover, this internet service expenditure must be more amount, due to it needs to provide its webstores online book ( electronic books and paper books) to sell and electronic library e-book lending service to global readers, 24 hours. Thus, internet service expenditure must be Amazon publish long-term influential transaction expenditure because, any electronic books and paper books, even e-library books borrow service and readers must need to pay visa card for borrowing book month service fee and purchase books from amazon publish e-publish webstores in any time every day.

Hence, Amazon publish must need have good management account strategy in order to predict whether different countries will have how many readers click to its different countries e-publish webstores to spend time to choose different authors books to buy or borrow to read from intenet channel. So, any countries readers budgeting number, readers reading habit behavior, e.g. US has about one million online readers click Amazon e-publish webstores , but it has only three thousands readers pay visa card to buy its ebooks and paper books from its Amazon electronic publish webstores, in this week , but next week, US has about seven thousands online readers click Amazon e-publish webstores, but it has three thousands readers pay visa card to buy its ebooks and paper books. Hence, it seems tha although this week has one million online readers click to Amazon publish electonic webstores to seek any books, but the book buyer number has only three thousands. Otherwise, although next week, it reduces three thousands e-readers click to visit Amazon e-publish webstores e-readers number , but it still keep same three thousand e-readers to choose to buy Amazon publish's books to read.

I assume that Amazon publish needs to pay a fixed internet service expenditure, e.g. US $500,000, but it design this e-publish webstores can help it to do its different countries e-publish webstores, their daily e-readers visiting number, daily electronic book and paper book sale number and daily e-readers visiting time statistics. It's electronic publish webstores can help it to record any countries' reading habits and reading taste , e.g. how many fiction , story books have sold in the week, how many non fiction books have sold in the week , e.g. business topic books have sold next week.

So, Amazon publish can use its e-publish webstores to gather above data in order to make author book topic sale choice, e.g. whether this week, US market ought sell how many consumer psychological topic book, US market ought sell how many management topic book next week. If this week US market can only sell one thousand consumer psychological topic book to compare its budget is less than one thousand consumer psychological topic books budget sale number reduces, e.g. in the week, there are two thousands readers choose to buy consumer psychological topic books from European market in this week. It implies that there are many European readers who like to read consumer behavior books recently. Hence, Amazon can attempt to concentrate on encouraging authors to write more consumer psychological books to let European readers to read within next several months.

Basic on above effects, Amazon needs to provide rapid internet service to European libraries, schools ,e-book partners to help them to promote Amazon consumer psychology topic books in order to let the European consumer psychological students, consumer psychology lecturers, consumer psychologists to know Amazon publish can provide more different topics concern consumer psychology research in order to increase Amazon 's consumer psychology book European market book buyers bumber.

As above case, I assume Amazon publish needs to pay a fixed internet service expenditure , e.g. US$500,000 per month. Amazon needs webstores to evaluate whether it is value, if it helps European schools, libraries organizations to pay internet fee, in order to let they can let many consumer psychology students and teachers and consumer psychologists to know that Amazon publish may have enough different consumer psychology books to be provided to European publish libraries, schools readers to read. For example, I assume next several month, Amazon publish needs to pay US two million internet service expenditure to global different European countries to help Amazon publish itself to promote its al different authors' consumer psychology topic books as well as it evaluates that it will sell different European countries; students , teachers and consumer psychologists readers, they have about three million readers at least choose to buy its one million consumer psychology topic authors; paper books and electronic books next several months as well as it also needs to evaluate whether it can earn more than US ten million at least royalty income after reducing author royalty from all European countries book markets.

Thus, if Amazon publish makes decision to help European countries schools, public libraries to pay internet expenditure to help it to advertise its one million consumer psychology topic authors electronic and paper books to sell. It must needs to pay fixed US$500,000 internet expenditure for Amazon publish its all e-bpublish webstores and it also needs to pay extra two million internet service expenditure for global all European countries libraries and schools per month. If next month, Amazon publish can earn more than US tem million at least royalty income after reducing author royalty from all European countries book market. Then, Amaozn publish ought attempt to make this internet service expenditure for all European schools, libraries organizations, if it had confidence to earn this royalty amount from European consumer psychology book readers, such as this Amazon publish.

On conclusion, , this Amazon publish organization case, it may attempt to apply management accounting science method to make book sale number budget, royalty income budget, even analysis to reader individual reading habit, book topic choices, book sale price evaluation in order to judge whether the kind or topic book ought concentrates on selling to which countries marekts, such as Amazin publish case, it also may choose different consumer psychology topic books to concentrate on selling to different European countries in next several months, if it can earn all European royalty income more than its internet service expenditure to European schools, libraries, then Amazon may attempt to make this decision.

Otherwise, it won't be good decision.

Hence, it implies that management accounting is one kind of business management science, it can apply number to help any organizations to do right or reasonable reason more accurate as well as it is different to traditional financial acounting, it only helps organizations to record and income and expenditure, earn or loss record function. Hence, management accounting may help any organizations to attempt implement useful or effective strategies in order to improve themselves performance.

How management accounting concept applies to investment

Can we apply management accounting concept to investment decision aspect? An organization's investment decision may make risk, so they need risk evaluation to decide whether the project can bring ehat benefit before they want any decisions. Risk management is the process of assessing, managing and mitigating losses . This applies to both business and investing risk management exists in many forms throughout the financial world, such as one individual investor decides to buy low risk government securities, instead of high yield corporate bonds in an example of risk managment companies and investors frequently use financial managment method like options, and future and strategies, like portfolio and investment diversification, in order to effectively manage risk.

For investment management strategy example, it is professional asset management of various securities, including shareholdings, bonds and other assets, such as real estate, in order to meet specified investment goals for the benefits of investors. Investors may be insurance companies, pension funds, corporations, charities, educational organizations or private invetors.

The term asset management is often used to refer to the management of investment funds. So managerial accounting is the process of identifications, measurement , analysis and interpretation of accounting information that helps business leaders make financial decisions and efficiently manage their day operation . The main objective of managerial accounting is to maximize profit and minimize losses . It is concerned with the presentation of data to predict inconsistencies in finances that help managers make important decisions, such as investment decision for Amazon publish book sale country market choice for which topic of books which are the most popular, in order to concentrate on selling the topic of books to the country market. So, Amazon publish needs to gather past different kinds for any one country, number data may include each author ebook and paper books sale prices, each author different book topic books sale number , in order t make which topic of book sale to which countries investment decision aims to increase readers number t o the country book sale market. So, Amazon publish may be apply these tools of management accounting to gather datas to concern book sale record. They may include: Financial accounting, financial statement analysis, book cost accounting, fund flow analysis , cash flow analysis, standard costing, marginal cost, budgetary control , management accounting tools.

● How to apply mental accouting method to predict investor behavior?

The main aim of management accounting to investment includes planning, controlling and evaluating. Thus, the advatanges to investment may include; better decision making, increase business efficiency, simplify financial statement, raises profitability, motivates employees, cost control, reliability. Hence, management accounting means " mental accouting", it is a concept in the field of behavioral economies. Mental accouting refers to the different values of person places on the same amount of money, based on subjective criteria, often with detrimental results. Mental accouting is a concept in the field of behavioral economies. Developed by economist Richard H, it contends that individuals classify funds differently and therefore are prone to irrational decision making in their spending and investment behavior. It refers to the different values people value on money, based on subjective criteria, that often has detrimental results, mental (managerial )accounting decisions and behave in financially counterproductive or detrimental ways, such as funding a low interest savings account when carrying learge credit card balances, to avoid the mental (managerial ) accounting bias, individuals should treat money as perfectly used tools when they allocate among different accounts, be it a budget account ( everyday living expenses), a spending account or a wealth account ( saving and investment). Also abother author indicates that managerial accounting means mental accounting, which appeared in the Journal of behavioral decision making, the begins with this definition, " mental accounting" is the set of lognitive operations used key individuals and households to organize, evaluate , and keep tracks of financial activities. He considers of how mental accounting leads to irrational spending and investment behavior.

- How mental ( managerial) accounting concept helps Amazon publish to make investment decision?

I believe that Amazon publish may apply mental accounting concept to help it to predict whether which topic of books will be the most popular to sell to the country market more accurately. The reason concerns that it can apply all data gathering to analyze whether past has how many readers paid visa to buy the topic of electronic or paper books to prepare to the country , e.g. in this year, Jan. it had 40,000 readers buy fiction electronic books and paper books from Amazon publish US market website to read , it had 100,000 readers buy fiction electronic and paper books to read in European market website and the year Feb. It had 70,000 readers paper books from Amazon publish US market website, it had 200,000 and paper books from Amazon publish European market website. Now, it is Mar. So, Amazon publish may make assumption that fiction (story) topic book is accepted to read by American and European readers, due to US fiction readers had increased 30,000 number in past one month and European fiction readers had increased 100,000 number in past one month.

However, US and European readers number data is not enough to evaluate whether US and European fiction readers number may still keep to increase. It depends on other factors, e.g. fiction e-book and fiction paper book sale price, if one author's ficton's ebooks and paper books rising prices whether it will influence US and European fiction book buyers make book purchas decision to the author's any fictions. So, Amazon publish need s to make the author's past different kinds of fiction books sale prices record in order to judge whether his fiction book's variable price ( changing price) will bring negative or positive impact to his readers' fiction book purchase decision. For exmaple, if the author (A)'s one fiction price increased 10% to ebook and paper book sale price between Jan and Feb. His fiction readers number won't be influenced to reduce, even his fiction readers number can still increase 10%. So, it implies that this author's fiction is attract or popular to US and Eurpopean fiction reader market. Amazon publish ought concentrate on helping this author (A) to advertise his fiction to let many US and European readers to know.Hence, it explains that Amazon publish may attempt to gather past every author individual writing book topic book sale proce whether it is increased or decreased how much %, book sale number in order to make book sale investment decision to concentrate on helping whom to advertise to sell to which book sale country market.

So, it seems that mental accounting concept can be applied to Amazon publish to help it to do any author individual book sale country market advertisement investment decision. For example, if Amazon publish can only spend US$10,000 advertieing expenditure to help author (A) to sell fictions to US and European both markets in Mar. , then it can help author (A) to increase 20% more fiction sale number to US and European both markets. This advertiscment expenditure is worth to spend for this author (A) in fiction market.

Hence, it implies that mental accounting concept can be applied to publish investment market, such as choosing which country to sell which topic of books, e.g. US sells more which fiction or European sells more fiction or Japan sells more management business topic books or UK sells more consumer psychology business topic books. All of these issues will be any publisher's important book sale market decision . It may influence their royalty income because if the publisher makes wrong decision to sell not popular topic books to the country market, e.g. in the month, US ought have many business topic readers to choose any business topic books to buy from any publishers, if the publisher makes wrong decision to find many fiction authors to help it to increase fiction stock to prepare to sell to US book market. Then, excess fiction stock may cause low fiction price ( fiction book supply or publisher's fiction stock number) is more than fiction book demand ( readers). Otherwise, it can not increase business topic books royalty inocme to US book market, because it has not enough different topic, such as management, consumer psychology , accounting, economy , marketing topic business books stock to be putted on book shelves to let US readers to choose when they visit US any book shops in the month.

On conclusion, it explains why mental ( managerial ) accounting has close relationship to influence customer behavior in behavioral economy view. Mental accounting is a management science or behavioral science tool to help any businessmen to make the most effective or the most reasonable busines decision in nowadays society.

Management science accounting concept how predicts market changing

Accounting aims to help any organizations to record whether the year has what kinds of expenditures, how much of every kind of expenditure finds what factors to cause the kind of expenditure needs to be spent too much in order to avoid excess spending, measurement profict or loss level why what factors cause the year had loss or profit growth in order to achieve long term performance improvement or avoiding loss. Hence, accounting system is not only for bookkeeping record financial performance aim. Accoungint may be one kind management science concept to be applied to explain why and how market changes in order to predict whether the company ought implement which strategies to grow up its business groth or increase clients number.

The question concerns why the organization can apply accounting concpet to predict how the market will change in order to avoid profit falls down or loss causes. I shall attempt to explain as below: For a watch product sale organization example, this watch sale compay own 100 expensive price watch brand products stock to prepare to sell, their sale prices are between US$3,000 to US$5,000 , so the watch brand prices are below than US$3000, they belong to low prices. It has 100 low price watch brand products stock to prepare to sell. Hence, every month, it keeps exact 100 high price of brand watch products stock and exact 100 low price of brand watch products stoc to prepare to sell. I assume this watch company can sell 100 low price watches and 100 high price watches in this month, but next month, it can sell 50 low price watches and 0 high price watches. Hence, it means that next watch , low prices watches sale number falls 50 number and high price watches sale numbe falls 100 number. It ensures that this company's profit may be influenced to fall by the high and low watch price client reducing number factor. However, this company still lacks data to know whether its competitors ; watch price is the main factor to influence its watch buyers number reduces or whether other factors influence its watch buyers number reduces, e.g. whether its high and low watchs are attractive or not attractive to high its watch design buyers number reduces or whether smart phone product invention influences watch users begin feel watchs have not be importnt to help them, because smart phones have time record function, they can replace traditional watch products or this month has higher unemployment rate, so it causes people do not like spend easily , in special, watch is not one kind essential product. Hence, it seems that this watch company can investigate its every month whether its low and high price watch stock sale record in order to attempt tp find whether what are the main factor to cause its watch sale number increases or decreases? I shall follow above every possible points to be investigated by accounting concept in order to explain why its watch low and high price customer number sudden reduces.

I assume that this watch company's last month and this month every high and low price watch brand's sale prices are stable. So, it seems that the influential factor won't be its " increasing sale price" to cause its high and low watch price customers number sudden reduces. If it gathered data concerns its watch competitots similar famous watch brands of general price range. It discovered their general sale prices do not have much difference between itself and their famous brnad of watchs. Also, it discovered that their these famous brand high and low price watch sale number is more than its sale number, e.g. the another similar famous watch brand company can sell 200 high price watchs and 200 low price watchs last month and 400 high price watchs and 400 low prcice watch this month. So, it seems that its high and low price of watch is not main factor to influence its watch sale number, because its high and low price watch's their price level had not changeed within these two months . Moreove, its watchs manufacture material costs had not increased within these two months. So, it ensures that its profit falls must not be influenced by watch manufacture cost increasing factor. Hence, it may depends on its accounting record to conclude the main factors influence its high and low price watch sale number reduces, they may include; poor watch design feeling to watch buyers factor, smart phones increasing need factor, unemploymenr rate rising factor.

The next step concerns how this watch company can apply accounting concept to find whether the main factor is poor watch design feeling factor, or smart phones are popular accepted to replace watch product feeling factor, or rising unemployment rate factor which one influences it s high and low price range watch sale number decreases can apply accounting cencept to investigate which is the main factor to influences its watch sale number decreased in this two months? I shall attempt to confirm this possibility as below:

Firstly, I assume this watch company's accounting record has marketing promotion expenditure, its expenditure includes advertisement fee, exhibition expense only, however, in its expenditure group accounting record, it has none design expenditure with these two months. Hence, it seems that its high and low price range fanous brands watches had not been improved by its improvement design skill method in order to improve their watch style, picture, shape, colour, function , design to satisfy watch buyers'changing watch fashion need in this competitive market. Hence, it seems that poor watch design feeling factor may be one main factor to influence its watch sale number decreases. It implies that accounting record may help it to find lacking new fashion watch design factor may be one main influential factor to cause watch buyers choose to buy other similar famous brands' watch products.

Next, whether accounting concept can help this firm to judge whether smart phones influences its watch sale number? I assume that smart phone products had been selling more than 10 years in this country in this case indicates US country. So, smart phones mus be its long time similar time seeing function competitors in US. I assume that its past 10 years high and low price range famous brand watches sale number must be more than these two months as well as it had not increases high and low price range of watches prices within this 10 years. Hence, it can depend on its past 10 years accounting record to judge whether smart phones product invention may influence watch buyers number decreases within these two months. basic on its past 10 years , accouniting record indicated that its high and lw price range watch sale number had been increasing, and it s watch price had not beedn increased and its markting advertisement promotion expense had been reducing much within 10 years. Thus, its past watching expense and watch price sale amount and profit accounting record may help it to conclude that smart phone product sale to US market is not the main factor to influence its recent high and low price range watchs sale number falls.

Finally, I shall explain whether this watch company may apply accounting concept to explain whether this month's high unmployment rate factor can influence geeral watch buyers' consumption desire as below:

I assume that this watch company employed 20 watch salespeople and their salaries range are between US$2,000 to US $4,000 per month in the first years . It operated till to this month total 20 years . However, its accounting record indicated that its watch salespeople number had been increasing from 20 to 50 number recently and their salaries range had been increading between US$3,000 to US$6,000 permonth. Hence, within these 10 years , this watch company employees number and their salaries range had been continue increasing. . It may depend on its past 10 years accounting record for salespeople salaries and employee number to reflect whether higher unemployment rate is the main factor to influence its watch sale number reduces.

I assume that within these 10 years, its unemployment rare was between 1% to 10%, in US society , although it may had 1% to 10% young people unemployed within 10 years. But, this watch company, I could also increased salespeople employees number and their salaries could also increase more significantly, even their salaries had not decreased in these 10 years. Hence, its accounting record of salsepeople salaries increasing trend , it may reflect this US watch market's local and overseas watch buyer individual buying watch desires ought not be influenced by slight rising unemployment rate factor, it is based on that this watch company will like to increase salespeople employee number, when it discovered there were many potential watch buyers visited its any watch shops every day within past 10 years. Hence, it implies higher unemployment rare won't influence watch potential buyer individual visiting to any one watch shops in US within these 10 years. So, this watch company's past salespeople salaries, employees number, and their salaries rising range record can reflect whether US higher unemployment ratio level can influence its recent high and low price range of watchs sale number decreases in US local watch sale market.

On conclusion, we can depend this watch company past 10 years accounting record to judge whether which one may be the most main fluential factor to influence its recent watch sale number reduces. I make the final conclusion that its poor watch design feeling factor ought be its main factor to influence its recent watch sale number reduces, due to it had not spend any design expenditure to improve its watch style in order to attract many watch buyers' choices within these 10 years. So, I believe that accounting concept can help any companies to revise whether what factos influence their businessess to be better or worse, instead of general booking record function.

Accounting trademark loyalty theory

In accounting theory view, any organizational goodwill or trademark, they are intangible asset because they can not touch, they are the company name. However, when the organization grows up a long time, ususally more than 10 years, if they are famous when consumers choose to buy the kind of product, they will must remember, then the organization's trademark or goodwill, company names will become the company's intangible asset in their balance sheet , financial report, e.g. Cock Coke soft drink, " Coca Coke" may be this soft drink company's trademaek , intangible asset to this soft drink company. Because any country's soft drinkers, they must remember Coca Coke brand soft drink before they make any brands of soft drink purchase choice. The reason may be Coca Coke soft drink . Its brand had been popular to be accept to be the first soft drink choice to any countries people. Hence, Coca Coke soft drink compnay must put is brand name to be intanginle asset in balance sheet, (B/S),

Why does Coca Coke's brand name ( intangible asset) value may increase or decrease in B/S. The reason is simple, when general consumers feel Coca Coka drink has better taste to compare other brands soft drinks. Then, they wil choose other brand soft driks to replace Coca Coke soft drink. So, if the year, Coca Coke's any taste of soft drinks sale number decreases, then it will feel its intangible asset of trademark value is devaluation, but if its soft drink sale number increases in this year. Its intangible asset of trademark value will increase in its B/S.

Hence, it explains why Coca Coke 's trade mark value can reflect its soft drink sale number whether it increases or decreases in the year. Thus, any firms mist hope their trademark , goodwill valuation can often increase every year. The question concerns how they can often keep their trademark valuation to increase? Can the firm increase sale number , it can represent that it has long term goodwill valuation increases? Can other factors influence or impact the firm's goodwill valuation changes? I shall attempt to give examples to explain these questions as below:

In fact, goodwill or trademark represents the company's famility whether how many consumers can remember its brand name , when they choose to buy the kind of product . So, if the firm's products are famous in market, Its products must have many consumers can remember it before they choose to buy the kind of product. So, product's familiar to publish,which ill be one measurement tool to judge whether what may be its goodwill valuation. If there are many consumers remember its brand before they want to buy the kind of products, the firm ought raise its goodwill valuation. It may make market research to enquire whether consumer will choose to buy which brand of product among several similar brands of product. It many people choose to prefer to buy its brand. Then, its brand familiar level to publis will be high grade. It may raise to goodwill valuation inB/S.

So, I think that goodwill fact valuation can not be measured by sale number or sale price or profit or loss amount. It ought be measured by market familiar level. If the product can have many people know its brand exitence in market. Then, its goodwill , intangible asset valuation ought be increased. Otherwise, if there are not may people know or they are familiar its brand existence in market. Then, its probable valuation ought need to decrease . Hence, any firms' goodwill valuation ought reflect their market familiar level for standard.

Do you feel firm goodwill valuation can represent its market value or product sale effort? In accounting principle, goodwill valuation must be measured by money. For example, Coca Coke brand goodwill valuation, in fact, Coca Coke had not pay another in B/S. Its goodwill valuation increases, it is not due to it pays its firm pays cash to buy goodwill. It is due to its capital increase. But, in fact, it does not need to increase cash to capital balance amount in B/S. Because coca Coke has not increase its cash amount, due to goodwill valuation increases. Its goodwill valuation increases, it supposes that is capital amount also be influenced to increase. So, Coca Coke 's goodwill valuation can not represent it has profit growth. Goodwill valuation only represents it has profit growth. Goodwill valuation only represents Coca Coke's present market valuw whether it increases or decreases in soft drink market. It is not actual cash available value. So, why firms need have goodwill valuation. The reason is simple. If one day, the firm hopes to sell its busines to another. When the another potential business buyer feels this firm's goodwill valuation is high. It may persuade b make business purchase decision more easily. because he believes that there are many people are famkliar this product brnad , then they will choose to buy theis product in preference . So, good goodwill valuation can build good business sale image to help the firm can raise business sale price to anyone . Such as Coca Coke soft drink goodwill case, if it can keep high goodwill valuation, then it can persuade any businesses buyers accept to pay high business purchase price. so, B/S goodwill valuation may help any famous business to sell to anyone in the high business sale price more easily.

Can goodwill valuation help the firm to predict market environment changes? For Coca Coke soft drink case example, I assume that it estimated its goodwill valuation is US 3 million , but this year, it estimates its goodwill valuation falls down to US one million. What factors influence Coca Coke feels its goodwill valuation reduces US two million in this year? I believe that is current year goodwill valuatin falls, it has relationship to whole global soft drink taste changes to global soft drinkers. The factors influence global drink makes taste changes , they may include:

global soft drinkers begin to dislike to choose to drink any brands of soft drink in preference, if they feel soft drink is one kind of bad health drink. They may choose to buy freash fruits to eat to replace any soft drink. I assume that the other soft drink brand companies' goodwill valuations are decrased. It means that if other soft drink brands' goodwill valuation can increase. Then, Coca Coke may believe that there are many soft drinkers prefer to choose other soft drink brands' soft drinks to drink. So, global soft drink markets still have competitive effort. Coco Coke nees to learn how to change its taste and let soft drinkers believe its soft drink can bring health to them to compare other soft drink brands. So, it seems that goodwill valuation also helps any organizations to eveluate how market changes to influence itself product sale effort. It explains why goodwill valuation is one kind of good market changing predictable tool t any businesses in accpunting concept, instead of sale business valuation measurement tool.

On conclusion, accounting principle or accounintg concept is not only be applied to bookkeeping financial record aspect. If the organization hopes to find what factors to influence its customer number or they hope to predict whether market will ought how to change to be netter or worse. It may attempt to investigate its past every year some kinds of expenditure amount record in order to find how any why the firm itself needed to pay more or less to the kind of expenditure. It aims to research what factors may influence its past and present expenditur changes in order to find whether what the most influential factors are influenced itself buyers number increases or decreases . Hence, accounting is one kind of makret research scientific method to any organizations.

Accounting science how predicts e-commerce consumer behavior

Cash e-commerce organizations apply accounting record to predict consumer behaviors? If it is true, how e-commerce organizations can use past accounting record to predict consumer behaviors? In general, e-commerce sale transactions must need any individual e-buyers to register higher address to their e-store in order to deliver products to any one-buyer homes. For Amazon e-commerce organization, when one China client buys a furniture from US Amazon e-commerce organization, when one China client buys a furniture from US Amazon e-store. The furniture is putted to Amazon US itself warehouse. So, when the China e-buyer pays visa to buy the furniture . He needs to register his address to amazon e-store. When amazon confirms that it can receive cash from the China e-buyer visa card, then amazon will deliver the furniture from US amazon warehouse to the China e-buyer home by plane.

So, amazon must have any e-buyer address record and the product sale price record for any one country e-buyer after it comfirms that the e-buye visa card has enough money to buy the product. Thus, amazon can apply past every online transaction to follow these data to do market research, they may include: which country person buys the product, what the product is, how much to the product price, how many of different product number e-buyer purchase within the year. So, amazon can collect all above data to analyze any one country has the highest e-buyer number,e.g. in the year, there ar one million US e-buyers number, there are two million China e-buyer number,which kind of products are the most popular, e.g. soap , computer, furniture, cloth, shoe, shirt, towel, electronic products etc. what the age range is, e.g. young , old, students , workpeople, they choose to buy the kind of product, how many number , the family buys the kind of product to the e-transaction, how many goods return number to the year total e-transaction, how many goods return number to the year total e-transactions.

Hence, amazon can gather all past every e-transaction data to prepare how to predict whether how every country e-transaction will consumer behavior to predict whether how every country e-transaction will influence consumer behavior will change next year in order to let it to prepare how to implement new market strategy,e.g. how to advertise its product, which countries need to spend more advertise to promote its products, evaluate whether amazon needs to spend how much advertisement expenditure to earn more e-sale transactions number to the targe sale country.

Why does amazon's any one e-transaction's accounting record assists it to predict consumer behavior? For china target e-buyers market example, when one Shanghai city e-buyer pays visa to buy one computer from amazon e-store, if the e-transaction can be accepted . Amazon can gather the e-buyer is living in China Shanghai city, which brand of computer , he chooses to buy, how much sale price to the computer, how many of computers number , he buys, how many e-transaction times to the China, Shanghai city buyer within the year. Hence, when amazon needs know where China target market has how many e-buyers number to every city, how many e-transaction return goods and refind number, which kinds of product are the popular to China e-buyers' purchase needs, which is the highest price and the lowest price sale level to China, Shanghai city target e-commerce market every e-transaction . Thus, when amazon collestc all above China, Shanghai past one year any individual e-transaction data, it can compare whether how its China, Shanghai city.

Nest year, e-buyers behavior change in order to analyze whether which kinds of product price ought need to reduce in order to attract many China e-buyers to click amazn webstores to pay visa to buy its products or which kinds of product price may increase, when the kind of product is popular to sell to China target market, or make out of e-stock shelf decision to the kind of product when Amazon discovers the kind of product is not accepted to buy in popular from its e-store. Thus, it seems that Amazon's past any one e-transaction accountning record can help it to analyze whether how every target market its e-buyer behavior is changing in order to change next year sale changing strategy is more reasonable . Hence, it explains why e-commerce organization's accounting record may help it to analyze how future market changes as well as record how every old e-buyer customer whether he/she will choose to buy the kind of old product again or buy new product, even not buy anything from Amazon e-stores this year.

Hence, any e-commerce organization's e-stores can apply online technology skil and accounting concept to help it to learn how to analyze every year post efficient countries' cities different e-buyer individual product behavioral choice in order to judge/revise whether it ought need to change to buy its products from its e-stores conveniently. So, any e-commerce organization explains why it can attempr to apply its post every accounting e-buyer sale transaction record to make every country consumer behavior marketing analysis to compare transaction visiting shop business model more easily, because visiting shop sale model can let the seller to sell its products in its shop, when it locates in the country. But e-commerce sale model can let the product can be sold to different countries more easily.

So, it seems that if the e-commerce organization can have good accounting record system to keep its past all e-transactions record can gather all data concerns any countries e-buyer individual address , how much sale price for the product, how many sold, and refund to the country e-buyers and the e-buyer age is young or old , male or female e-buyer purchase habit.

Can the e-commerce organizatin predict consumer behavior if it implemented inefficiency accounting record system? Firstly, we need to know good or right accounting record system can help the organization to track or find past any transactions more easily. So, if the organization has none good accounting record system , its accounting record system can not be improved efficiently. Then, its accounting record may bring wrong sale price record, wrong profit ( over -profit) or less profit or wrong loss ( over loss) number record. Then, this wrong sale transaction record may mislead financial performance to publis to know, e.g. current year, its sale performance is improved, but in fact, its current year sale number is less than last year sale number. Consequently, this organization can not predict its consumer behavior. Whether know to change exactly, due to it often has wrong sale number record, e.g. higher or lesser sale price record, and more or less sale number may influence its gross profit earns high amount, even if its any kinds of expense record is more orless, it will influence its net profit is more or less or less is more or less, for example, if the organization earns US one million dollar prodict this year, but due to it smore sale number transaction to cause over profit. So, its financial performance report indicated its earned US two million dollar. So, it believes its buyers number can increase, if its sale prices do not change. This wrong financial performance report many mislead it has good consumer behavior in this year. Then, it will continue implement its old marketing strategy. Consequently, its next year financial performance may be caused worse to compare present. So, it implies that wrong financial record may cause wrong consumer behavior judgement.

Can robots perform management accounting analysis tasks

Our future will experience artificial intelligent development stage. Nowadays, we had had some tasks which can be done by robots, e.g. warehouse delivery, restaurnt kitechen dish cleaning tasks, transport tasks, even non drive manual auto driving tasks, shopping center service etc. cleaning or customer service simple jobs duties. If one day, robots cab be applied to do office tasks, e.g. accounting record tasks, they may replace account clersk, even accountants to deal simple accounting record tasks, even complicate management account analysis tasks in office working environment. If future robots can be developed to help accounts clerks as well as accountants to do simple bookkeeping debit and credit every income ot expense transaction record in order to analyze marketing research tasks, then it brings this question: Can future robots replace accounts clerks and accountants to do their accounting tasks in any organizations. I shall attempt to research the relationship between robots and accounting tasks questions as well as whether robots will bring what social influence if robots can replace future human to do any simple and complex accounting tasks for any organizations.

What is need for development of artificial intelligence to accounting tasks aspect? The first computer language used to create artificial intelligence is USP. This language is quite flexible and extensive . Features such rapid prototyping and macro are very useful in creating AI. LISP is a language that makes complex tasks simple. So it seems that it is possible tobots can learn human to do any kinds of accounting tasks, e.g. financial account record, audit check, management account analysis etc. different kinds of acounting tasks for financial , management account, audit check functions in any organizations.

However, scientists believe that artificial intelligence can help accountants be more productive and efficient. Robotic process automation RPA) allows machines or AI workers to complete repetitive, time-consuming tasks in business processed, such as document analysis, handling that are plentiful in accounting . AI can also significantly reduce financial fraud and maintenance accounting errors. Hence, the stages of AI development to accoutning industry, they may include: internet AI, business AI, perception AI, and autonomous AI ., Internet AI is thr simplest stage of AI, business AI has a limted memory, perception AI. This is the first stage in the future of AI. A key feature of this perceptive form of AI is the ability to compile and draw from past experiences, much like human to accounting tasks.

The design phase is essentially in literative process comprising all the steps releveant to building the AI or machine learning model, data acquisition, exploration, management and analsis tasks. So, it seems that future robots may be developed to help human to do simple and complex accounting tasks. Combining AI with other technologies, such as robotic, process automation can follow accountants to redirect the time that they used to spend on multiple tasks, toward performing high-value, high -impact taaks. Adding AI to accounting operation can also increase output quality by miniizing human errors. So, AI and automation won't be replacing finance and accounting professionals in the foreseeable futue.

On the contrary, as AI automates many aspects of business, there is a bug opportunity for accounting and finance professsionals to upskill themselves to meet the requirements of the 21 centurey. For AI audit task aspect, AI enables the analysis of a full populatin of data and can identify outliers or expectations. By making it possible for auditors to work better and smarter. AI will help them to optimize their time, enabling them to use their human judgement to analyze a boarder and deeper set of data and documents.

Can AI be used in auditing and accounting ? In the assurance practice, AI is being used to perform auditing and accounting prcedures, such as review of general ledgers, tax compiance, preparing workpapers, data analytic, expense compliance, fraud accounting skills. So, it seems that future AI can replace market research analysists, compensation and benefits managers , instead of financial accountants, management accountants an auditors in any organizations.For bookkeeping clerks position example, these simple account jobs are expected to decrease, by 8% 2024, and it's non surprise because most bookkeeping is getting automated if it has not been as of now, Quickbook, Peachtrss etc. accounting software that does not need any more, because robots do not need any kinds of accounting software to help them to do any simple or complex accounting tasks.

How has teachnology changed the accounting industry? Computers and accounting softeare has changed the industry complexity, with but when robots develop, it will change global accountancy professional more complex. Can robots replace accountants? Automation had brought significant changes the accounting profession over the last decaed. When some tools have made accountants lives easier. However, since robots invention, it developed these tools have also created a false debate about whether automation will overtake the global accounting industry compexity and make accountants irrelvant . The question should not be whether automation will take over accounting, but where its rreal value lives.

In fact, I believe that no any software can match the critical thinkning and trusted counsel that a human advisor offes, as valued accountants, have become business partners, where software is limited to evaluating concrete inputs, accountants can understand clients business goals and observations voice to make decisions. This allows them to serve as advisors to their clients, whether by adjusting business models in real time, or managing emplyer wellbeing . Sok, future AI development ought not replace human accountant's this kind of skill more easily.

● How robotic process automation impact on accouting industry changes?

Searching for methods to efficiently perform accounting tasks can be dated book to the 1950 s, when process mechanisation involved the use of punched cards to store and retrieve transaction data ( Keenoy, 1958). Since then IT ad automation have transtormed the way accountants collect, store, process and share data through a variety of tools ( Ellis, 1986); Kaye, Nicholson, 1992; Rom, Rohde, 2007). However, robotis process automation is a technology solution that allows end-users to comfigure a software robot to use existing applications to perform accounting transactions manipulate data and communcation with other systems ( introduction to robotis, 2015).

Software robots can be easily programmed or trained to perform repetitive, rules-based , high volume operations by replicating human actions when accessing multiple systems, applications, and documents ( Embracing robotic automation 2018). Hence, robotic accounting software can bring cost reduction to counting and finance tasks, e.g. one robotic accounting software can replace two to five full time accounting clerks, increased process speed, software robots perform routime tasks faster than employees would manage mamually ( Cacity, Willcocks, 2016) . They do not get distracted or tried and thus avoid delays, cycle times decreases significantly improved process control and performance visibility, e.g the collected analytical information is much more detailed and can be used for audit and compliance checks, higher quality data ( accuracy, consistency, compliance), e.g. robots can validate the data before reporting or using them future. Assuming that the appropriate rules have been thoroughly tested beforehand, data inaccuracy and quality risk decrease fill tracking and logging robots' action make internal and external audits easier and reduce compliance risks, continuous operation 24 hours a day, or none working day limits. So, robots are applied on accounting task aspect, it can bring positive impact on employees, repetive tasks taken over by robots release employees' times. They can shift their focus on higher value added tasks, solve employee morale proble,. Any accounting department staffs may feel tired when they need over time works, often but robotic accounting staff won't have tired or bored feeling.

However, robotic process, automatin may be applied on these accounting tasks aspect, they may include: internal control period end clising, general ledger, subledgers, closing , validatin of journal entries, low-risk accounts, reconsiliation, consolidation, reporting-monthly , quarterly close, internal performance and management reportng aggregating and analysing financial and operational data, external statutary report, accounts receivable and payable record-maintaining updating customer/supplier data, creating processing, posting payment, collections, billing, matching invoices, aganist sales and purchase orders, cash management, general accoutning, inter-company transactions, inventory accountancye, travel and expenses reimbursement request, audit and document expense report, payroll, stock keeping, fixed asset accouting record, tax accounting. So, the general simple accounting tasks robots will have effort to finish.

- Can robots perform the same management accounting analytical decision making skills to human management accountants tasks?

Although, robots can perform simple bookkeeping audit accounting tasks, but whether complex management accounting analytical and decision making tasks, robots can do the same level of management accounting analytical, decision making tasks to human management accountants?

I shall attempt to answer this question. How robots impact of mental accounting in valuation? No retailers show this price without considering the " 99" in end. This indicates to our mind that the price is cheaper. Its popularity can be verified gas stations all around the world. The difference between robots mental accounting issue and management accountants.

The Anchoring theory was used to verify its possible impacts on capital venture tech finds decisions, during equity trading for an initial investment starting. Management accountants ususally arrange 68% of the finds use-valuation as a basic, when 21% proposed other methods . But still use valuation and only 11% of the investors said they did not consider valuation at allo. the context considered that the human management accountant will consider that the investment would be made in a startup in early stages. That is with little or any real accounting information can image the amount of uncertainty that exists in the type of analysis? Moreover, why do even experienced fund managers invest based on an impossible calculation> In simplity, it explains that human management accountant in order to do any investment decision. Although robotis will use alaytic mind more than calculating to estimate any investment risk in order to make investment decsion for any organizations. AI's analytic skill and human management accountant calculation risk skill be their difference on how dealing management accounting investment risk issue aspect. Even, the difference between human management accountant and robotic management accounting automation is their robotic management automation can apply mental accounting theory to judge consumer behavioral choice.

It is a new model of consumer behavior is developed using a hyrod of psychology and microeconomics. The deveopment of the model starts with the mental coding of combinations of risks and losses using the prospect theory value finction. Then, robotic management accounting automatin can attempt to evaluate of consumer purchase for the product is modeled using the new concept of " transaction utility", e.g. one family electronic firm, it is seeling rice cooker, television radio, household electronic products, it can learn how to mental accounting method to help this houseold electronic product firm to predict how any why its different kinds of household electronic products choice may change to its consumer behavior next week, e.g. robots can gather wlectronic product competitors prices data to compare itself company's same kinds of electronic product data e.g. rice cooker prices and its competitors' rice cookers prices, whether its high price , rice cookers price factor or other factors influence its rice cookers sale number decreases in this week. Consequently robotic management accounting software may help this household elecronic product company to analyze whether what are the actual factors to influence its rice cookers prces reduce in this week. It is human management accountants feel difficult to collect past price data in order to make accurate consumer behavior changes, prediction or find whther are the main factors to influence product sale number increases or decreases.

Hence, future robotic management accounting automation can learn the valuation of purchase modeled using the new concept of transactin utulitym such as this houseold electronic product case, robotic management accounting automation many learn the household budget process ,the characterization of mental accounting, in order to find whether household purchase behavior to the company's products whether what the main factors may influence its household producys sale number increases or decreased.

On conclusion, future robots can do simple bookkeeping, audit check , general daily accounting tasks, even robots can also do complex management accounting tasks, they can learn how to apply mental accounting knowledge to gather the company's past all every month different price variable data, sale number, in order to conclude whether what are the main factors to influence the kind of product sale number increases or decreased more accurately to compare human management accountants in any organizations.

Applying HR management accounting learns consumer behavior

Managerial accounting purposes to be used by management in "making by business decision: It includes product caost, budget , forecast and various financial analysis consumer behavior is the series of behaving of patterns that consumers follow before making a purchase through consumer behavior, you can also earn how customers interact with and the year products. So, any organizations may attempt to find any management account past year past per month transaction records to bring consumer behavioral change predictiver knowledge, it can help future decisions about product creation more easily.

Hence , the management accoutning knowledge focuses the process of creating organization goals by identifying, measuring, analyzing, interpreting and communicating informations to managers is call management or manerical accounting. Management accounting focuses on all accounting aimed at informing management about operational business metics. Also, any managers may attempt to gather past product number presentation date to find whether what the main factors can influence consumer buying behavioral change in its any kinds of products, the level of motivation also affects the buying behavior of customers, e.g. whether the products' sale prices sight rise, to influence customer number reduces, or whether the product's traditional old design is not more attractive or popular to accept to compare other linds of competitors' similar product design, or whether the kind of product is not popular to be accpeted to use, the another how invention of similar product ot the market is recession , it need to change another new sale market, if replaces its existence etc. different factors.

Hence, management accounting can help managers to attempt to gather past the product's sale and production past data to carry on analyzing whether what the main factor to influence its customer number reduces or increases in other to improve its sale strategy.

● Computer sale applies management accounting to predict consumer behavior

For computer sale product example, the computer saller may attempt to apply management accounting to analyze why computer buyer behavioral changes, e.g. a study of consumer behavior will reveal what kind of consumers buy computers, could they buy for home and personal use or for office, what features , they look for, what benefit o they seek including post purchase service, huw much they are willing to pay how many they are likely to buy . All of these computer buyer individual purchase behavioral analysis, the computer seller can follow its different models of laptops, desttops, prices, sale number, house or office ise design kind etc. data to research and analyze and predict hether future computer buyer individual need will how changes, in order to prepare and learn how to design new kinds of desktops and laptops to raise competitve effort.

In fact, in computer industry, the factors may influence computer buyer behavioral change, they may include core technical features, past purchase services, price and payment, conditions, physical appearanre, value added features and connectivity and ability are the main seven factors that are influencing consumers' laptop purchases choices.

- How can the laptop computer seller applies management accounting data to analyze whether which is the main factor to influence laptop buyer behavior changes?

for last month, I assume that laptop model (A) laptop computer sale price si per US$1000 and it can sold 1000 number and laptop model (B) laptop computer sale price is per US$1,500 and it can sold 2000 number.SO, it implies that although laptop model (B) computer sale price is more than US$500 to compare laptop model (A) computer, but the model (B) laptop computer can still sell more than 1000 number fo compare model (A) laptop computer last moth. It seems that model (B) laptop's attractive dsign, more fuction, rapid connectivity and mobility and attrative physical appearance main factors may influence laptop (B) model computer products sale number is more than laptop (A) model computer products last month. But, in this month, it has significant change between laptop model (A) and laptop (B). In this month, laptop modle (A) and laptop model (B) prices are not changes, but laptop model (A) can sell 3,000 number and laptop model (B) can sell only 500 number. Consequently, their sale numbers have significantly changes, laptop (A) can increase more 2,000 sale number, but laptop model (B) can decrease 1,500 sale number between these two months. It explains that although it seems that laptop (B) model has possible own attractive physical appearance, and rapid connectivity and mobility, more function to cause it can sell more than laptop (A) model computer produc. But, it ensures that all of anh one these possible factors can not help it to raise sale number in long time. It means that laptop model (B) may have other factors to influence itss sale number, e.g. other brand of laptop computers' physical appearance, more function, connectivity and mobility , features , even they can provide better value added sale service, repair service, product delivery service, feature to compare this brand of laptop seller, or its laptop model (B) buyers had lost confidence to use its laptop model () computer products, because they often need to repair and pay extra repair service fee frequently, e.g. one year has one time to two times at least per year. SO, their past poor frequent repair experience influences they choose to buy other brand of laptops. Otherwise, why laptop model (A) computer products number can sell more 2,000 number , the factor may include non rising price, none frequent past repair experiences to any one model (A) laptop buyer , their individual psychological positive feeling factor . So, it seems that gather these two laptop model (A) and model (B) past sale number, sale price data to conclude whther what main factors may influence its model (A) and model (B) laptop sale number to increase or decrease in long term.

However, this laptop computer seller can not only depend on the gathering these two months short time sale numbers ans sale prices data to model (A) and (B) laptops, in order to make the final conclusion concerns whether what the main factor can influence model (A) and model (B) laptop product sale number changes absolutely. It must need to continue to keep the long time management sale umber and sale prie data record for laptop (A) and (B) in order to conclude whether what the most accurate influential factor is that it can influence laptop model (A) and B() sale number both change in order to implement the improvement strategy for them both.

- Management accounting data can also help this laptop seller to predict future market development or whether which market will have high sale effort, e.g. Japan laptop sale market may have the highest market share ratio, among different Asia countries, or Germany laptop sale market may have highest market share ratio among different European countries next year. For example, in the last year, this laptop computer seller had sold 50,000 laptops to Japan computer market, it has sold 500,000 laptops to China computer market, it has sold 100,000 laptops to US computer market and 50,000 laptops to Germany computer market, in this year. its these laptop markets sale prices are not changed, it has sold 200,000 laptops to japan computer market, it has sold 400,000 laptops to China computer market, it had sold 200,000 laptops to US computer market and 200,000 laptops to Germany computer market . Hence, it ensures that Germany laptop market has increased 4 times sale number from last year and Japan has increased 4 times sale number from last year. Otherwisem China laptop sale number has decreased 100,000 laptops from last year and US laptop sale number has increased 1 time from last year. So, it can imply that Germany and Japan future laptop sale number may grown rapidly to compare US and CHina laptop sale markets. It also indicates this sale trend also may help this laptop computer to attempt to find whether what factors may influence its US and China laptop sale number fells down,e.g. whether this local laptop choices increasing factor, it laptop physical appearance is not more attraction, or slow connectivity and mobility speed ,even their model (A) and () laptop prices are higher to compare US and China local other similar brands of laptops prices.

In summary, I believe that management accounting technique can be attempted to apply to help any kinds of products to find whether what main factor(S) to influence their product sale number changes, it is one kind of good data gathering and analytical tool to help any businesses to attempt to predict consumer behavioral changes.

Organization management accounting strategy

What is organization management accounting strategy? As its most basic an organization management accounting strategy is a plan that specifies how your business will allocate resources, e.g. money, labour, and inventory to suppoty production, marketing, inventory and other business activities. IN general, the foure organizational straategy and the culture of the organization categorized into four types: Adhocracy, market and hierarchy.

The purpose of an organization management accounting strategy can be defined as the direction an organization takes with the aim of achieving future business success. Strategy sets out how an organization intends to employ its resources, including the skills and knowledge of its people as well as financial and material assets, in order to achieve its mission or overall targets. So, the key element of an organizational strategy may include: define vision, create mission, set objectives, develop strategy, outline approach, get down to tactics. However, an organizatinal strategy plan is an organizational management activity that is used to set priorities, focus energy and resources, strengthen operations, ensure that employees and other stakeholders are working toward common goals established agreement crowd intended outcomes/ results, and access organizational missions.

Adhocracy strategy is a form of business management accounting that emphasizes individual initiative and self organization in order to accomplish tasks. This is in contrast to bureaucracy which relies on a set of defined rules and set hierarchy in accomplishing organizational goals. The term was popularized by Alvin Toffler in the 1970s. Examples of adhocracy include most project or marix organizations. Among private-sector organizations, high technology firms, particularly young firms facing fierce competition are sometimes organized as adhocracies. However, important examples of adhocracy do exist in government. Hence, adhocracy is a flexible, adoptable and informal form of organization that is defined by a lack of formal structure that employs specialized multidisciplinary trams grouped by functions. Adhocracy is characterized by an adoptive , creative and flexible behavior based on non-performance. Adhocray culture in a business context, is a corpoate culture based on the ability to adapt quickly to changing conditions. Adhocracies ar characterized by flexibility, employee empowerment and an emphasis on individual initiative.

The five basic marketing strategies may include: product, price and promotion and people in management accounting strategy aspect. They are key marketing elements used to position a business strategically. A market strategy refers to a business's overall game plan for reaching prospective consumers and turning them into customers of their products and services. For example, the BSC business 2 customed marketing strategies may include : social networks and viral marekting, paid media advertising, internet marketing, email marketing, direct selling, point-of-purchase marketing, co-branding, cause marketing, conversational marketing. Hence, marketing strategy or management accounting strategy is a long term toeard looing approach and an overall game plan of any organization or any business with the foundemental goal of achieving a competitive advantage by understanding the needs and wants of customers.

Hierarchy strategy describes a relations of corporate strategy and sub-strategies hierarchically and logically consistent at the level of vision, mission, goals, and metrics , e.g. HR strategy (human resource strategy), to general, the three levels of strategy are: corporate level strategy, this level answers the foundamental question of what you want to achieve, business unit level strategy focuses on how you've going to grow.

The management accounting strategy planning hierarchy is the organization's mission and vision both of ,which should be long-lasting and motivating. At the base of the hierarchy are the shorter term strategies and tactics that unit members will use to achieve the vision. So, the basic levels of management accounting strategy are: corporate, business, functional and operational level strategy. The strategic hierarchy aims to be concept used to understand the different types of strategy decision made in a organization, e.g. michael porter , three generic strategies ( cost leadership, differentation, and focus) that can be implemnted at any organizations. So, hierarchical levels of strategy managment accounting may be concerned with selection of which is the right generic strategy to implement, sale method, such as low product sale price, lot differentiation of product choice, and focus an main product feature market sale methods etc.

● The relationship between organizational management accounting strategy and avoiding resource waste

If an organization can implement good managment accounting strategy whether it can assist it to reduce any organizational internal resource waste, e.g. exceed human resource employment cost, facility used cost, using cost, efficient administration or management cost etc. essential organizational cost. Because any organizations must need to use resources in order to achieve efficient providivities, service activities, if the organization can implement effective strategy in order to measure its performance, whether strategy can assist it to judge how to avoid not essential resources spending. Can efficient strategy help organizations to avoid to waste resources? I shall attempt to explain as below:

Whether formal strategy implement can avoid formal technical measurement of scale and concentrates on the loca resource mobilization using aspect os small, medium and large organization? What does resource mobilization strategy mean? Resource mobilization refers to all activities involved in sesuring new and additional resources for your organization. It also involves making better use of and maximizing , existing resources.What are the stepd in resource mobilization?

Firstly, any organizations need to plan od designing a resource moilization strategy and action plan, secondary , finding key elements of a resource mobilization strategy, thirdly,act of practical step to implementatin, fourth identify, fifth step, engagement, sixth step, negotiate, eventh step, manage and report, final step, communicating results.

What are the source of resource mobilization to any organizations? For example includes spreading flyers, holding community meetings, and recruiting volunteers. Material may include financial and physical capital, like office space, money, equipment, and supplies . Human resources, such as labour experience, skills and expertise in a certain field.

How does an entrepreneur mobilize resources? To exploit opportunities, entrepreneurs monilize and recombine a variety of resources, such as financial capital ( e.g. cash, ot loan from a bank , human capital e.g. skills from a employees, and social capital e.g. information obtained from social contracts. Hence, the overall objectives of the resource mobilization strategy is to securce the necessary funds to deliver on the source mobilization strategic outcomes. To achieve this accurate resource used number and expenditure budget and emergency appeals will need sufficient preditable and contrributions. So, the aim of resource mobilization strategy outlines how secretariat will organize the process of prioritising, plannin, selecting projects, monitoring: broadening the resource channels, as well as coordinating with staffs for mobilising and effectively utilizing resources.

So, the genesis of resource mobilization strategy is a good, solid strategic plan, it should articulate activities that are more routine in nature and can be finded through the organizational internal efficient resource mobilization. Resource mobilization refers to all activities involves in securing . These new directions or new business opportunities are pursued using a distinct resource mobilization strategy .

On conclusion , an efficient resource mobilization plan is a term resource mobilization, it refers to all activities undertaken by an organizations to secure new and additional financial, human and material resources to advance its mission. Inherent in efforts to mobilize resources is the drive for organizational sustainability . So, resource mobilization is about an organization getting the resources that are needed to be able to do the work it has planned. Resource mobilization is more that just fundraising, it is about getting a range or resources from a wide range of resource providers for donors, through a number of different mechanisms. How does an entrepreneur mobile resources? To exploit opportunities, entreprensurs mobilize and combine a variety of resources, such as financial captial , e.g. cash or loans from a bank, human capital e.g. skill from an employee and social capital e.g. information obtained from social contract.

Why do organizations need resource mobilization strategy? The reasons may include: The principles of resource mobilization wih examples, it focuses on forging partnerships built on trust and mutual accountability . So, as to attract adequate and more predictable contributions, with the future goal of sustainability, it refers to all undertaken by an organizatin to secure new and additional financial , human and material resource to advance its mission, in efforts to mobilize resources is the drive for organizational sustainability, community mobilization is the process of bring together as many stakeholders as possible to raise people's awareness of and demand for a particular programme to assist in the delivery of resources and services, and to strengthen community participation for sustainability an dself -reliance, resource mobilization is often referrred t as " new business creaating chance" , the organization has a strong, yet flexible structure , such as writing proposal how to spend the least respurce expenditure in order to achieve the most satisfactory effective result to the organization.

Hence, developing a resource mobilization strategy plan , as the source of new business opportunities to the social and behavioral change considerations must be needed the organization as well as resource mobilization target at a minimum level should be needed to raise at transformational change happen on the ground and advocate for the products and may have to develop new business proposal.

● Can resource mobilization change improve organizational performance?

I believe that resource mobilization can help any organizations to change or improve performance to the better, even the best. I shall explain as below:

What are the sources of organizational change? Change originates in either the external or internal environments of the organization. External sources include political, social, technological or economic environment, externally motivated change may involve government action, technology development, competition , social values and economic variables.

How do organizational resources affect change? Results indicate that organizations possessing greater stocks of historically valuable resources were much less likely to engage in adaptive strategic change, but also that this resoure-driven towards change tended to have a even beneficial effect on performance . Wonder of organizational change management is easier spoken about than achieved by resource mobilization strategic in possible? Can create enterprise level value by effective process for resource allocation?

The key to success involves managing organizational change , so it leads to real and lasting improvements, tailoring to resource allocation how mobilization strategy. So, nowadays, organizational capacty for change: Increasing change capacity and avoiding change overload, organization, today risk is overcommitting resources, resulting in an overload condition wih which it how allocates its resources to tbe used efficiently or inefficiently. For example, on new government regulations, ne products development or growth aspect, organizational change efforts often run into some form of human resistance. First, management staffed its human resource departments with spend most of that time in efficiency. So, whether how organizational change is better, it depends on how it changes its old resources, e.g. human resource, facility, equipment resources, even management time resources to change new improvement resources change to be better . It means providing the resources, budget, authority, credibility and commitment for the effort to truly organizational change on improvement.

- Why does organizational resource budget need?

For example, managing a human resource department involves budget planning and execution . The human resources budger refers to the finds that how HR allocates to all HR processes. Unit should include in an HR budget. It may include: number of employees, projected for next year, benefits cost increases or decreases, salary cost increases or decreases, projected turnover rate, calculation, actual cost incured in the current year, new employee welfare benefits. programs planned, other changes in policy, business strategy , it may impact costs on HR cost aspect. So, an organization needs to budget whether it will have how much on what kinds of resources spending aspect, including human resources, facility, equipment and water , electricity etc. natural resource , it budget is a tool used for planning and controlling financial resources. It is a guideline for future plan of action, espressed in financial terms within a set of period time, knowing organization's priorities, objectives and goals helps it prepare organization resource budget.

Effectively leveraging people and budget, resource management is critical for organizations to ensure . They are optimizing and allocating resources to the right initiations, e.g. from a human resource perspective, the data needed to create a new budget include the following number of employees, working arrangement tasks time, management time, employee salary cost, due to costs that only impact the human resource department and impacts the entire organization both aspects. So, efficient HR cost budget can help refine goals that reflect realistic resources and how memebers of the organization to use fund because employee retirement can be expensive and it can b increased or decreased expense in any time, when the month needs increase or decrease employees number to any departments. It depends on whether tasks rate is needed to increase or decrease. So, an organization's HR cost budget can help how it makes the most accurate HR resource expenditure.

Organizational facility, equipment, shop, office, warehouse space resource budget why is important. Office space is as an enabling resource, equipment and furniture to enhance the organization's ability to achieve efficient operations and activities of the best organizational performance. In view of this analysis, facility planning personal would be one important factor to influence whether the organizatin can spend the least expenditure to use its resource. During business growth, any facility equipment, office , shop, warehouse space must increase , moreover staff puts increasing number on existing resources, so be sure to budget in order to make another option is to least equipment instead of buying it, whether you need moving insurance for important equipment and machinery, set budget to help prevent overspending.

All of the tasks that are include in maintaining a facility, such as equipment maintenance and building facilities whether are needed to improve, facility oversight, warehouse and special equipment whether is qpproriate space for customer service and uses resource dynamic of an organization's work patterns with work. It depends partly on the resources an organization is willing to invest or not, when it feels this facility resources are very important to influence its performance.

● What does organization office , shop , warehouse space resource management strategy?

Organization and using space must be land resource, if the organization can manage how to use its space in efficiency, then it can improve service performance or productive efficiency. Space management can be defined as a practice where an organization manages its physical space invnetory which includes tracking , control, supervision and utilization, planning of the space available. So, space management is the mangement of an organization's physical space inventory. Ths involves the tracking of how much space an organization has managing occupancy information and creating spatial plans. So, one efficient space resource using organization, it needs to undertake annual property assessment reviews, leverage individual projects to drive portfolio evoluation applya planning methodology on all project rises, utilize planning to define direction and scope focus on mathematics before graphics, define and collect only the required data on warehouse, shops, office, buildind space using aspect. For example, a space management ffice can give the organizatin an accurate picture of how many employees , it needs to have space for an average day, and show it the trends of demand for this space across weeks and months. This can help the organization to determine how many permanent desks could be converted to hot desks in office, warehouse or shop , saving space. For example, space managementin retail aspect, it is the process of managing the floor space adequately to facilitate the customers and to increase the sale. Shop space management is very crucial in retail as the sales volume and gross profitability depends on the amount of space used to generate those sales. Space management is a multi-step process that requires data gathering, analysis , forecast and strategizing. In prective, it involes creating a space management system that occupants throughout your organization, so whether the organization realizes it or not, every organization needs to know how to manage its space one way or another , if it hopes to improve its service or productive performance. Make use of these strategic space management and planning techniques, efficient and an unplanned, unmanaged office is not likely to magically transofrm into a well organized of productivity. So, space management is the management of an organization's physical space inventoty , employee working environment, shop product putting sheleves locatin, equipment, desk putting location. All of this tangible space physical factor may influence overall organizational service and/or productive performance and /or sale performance. So, space may be an organization's land usng resource because any organization's land using space must be limited size, they must have land space using shortage challenge if their products stock number increases, but warehouse space can not increase or shop products shelves number can not increase, but product sale number increases.

● The relationship netween organization behavior and resource using management accounting

Has organizational behavior and resource spending, they have close cause and effect direct relationship ? When one organization can perform better, whether it represents that it must spend much resource to use or when it perform poor, it represents that it must not spend much resource to use. Organizational behavior is a field of study that investigates the impact that organizational psychology and human resource management, the cause and effect relationship. How organizational behavior effects an oganization? Organizational behaviors propose that inventives are motivational factors that are crucial for employees to perform well. It changes the way people make decisions, e.g. decision to increase or decrease resources to use, when the organization feels that it has resource shortage or excess. However, businesse that are able to encourage risks in decision making within the company culture can enhance innovation and creativity.

In fact, organizational behavior has four main elements, people, structure, technology and external environment. So , tangible and intangable resources may influence organization behavior when it is needed to change by management, e.g. human behavior in a work environmen and determines its impacts on job structure, performance, communication, motivation, leadership etc. for example, when the manager has less time to prepare how to organize this meeting process to his client. His short managing meeting plan time , intangible time resource, it can influence his business proposal to be either accepted or rejected to this client. So , time resource whether it is enough or not. It can influence this manager's client proposal meeting whether it is accepted or rejected in possible.

Every employee behavior can determine the importance of group departments in business productivity. So, it seems that resources whether they are enough , they can impact on employee's performance. As a result, managers are able to maintain better relation with their employees by effective utilization of human resource. So, cause and effect relationship plays an important rolw in how an individual is likely to behave in a enough tangible and intangible resource provided or not enough organization.

Modern organizational behavior is characterised by the acceptance of a human resource model, e.g. whether the plant can provide enough productive equipment facility and space shelf for product putting location in order to raise or improve logistic transport efficiency in warehouse. So, plant warehouse space management and shelf putting location productive equipment facility these tangible resource factors may influence warehouse productive performance. It seems that tangible resource provision amount and space management or intangible resource time management resource, they have close relationship to influence organizational behavior. Consequently, it can achieve the result either performance improvement or worse performance. So, resource and performance organizations , they ought have cause and effect relationship in resource management mobilization strategy view.

- How applying artificial intelligent management accounting solution accounting challenges

One of the biggest challenges for management accountants nowadays is the preparation to face globalization in local and global market. Globalization competition is changing government regulation and innovation in technology had to change in the market environment which have greater impact to an organization. The role of managemet accounting to AI, it may help managers to make any management strategy decision, e.g. evaluate sale price is the most reasonable, sale market choice, customer age target evaluation etc. within any organizations. Also known of cost accunting, management account of the process of identifying, analyzing and communicating information to managers to help to achieve business goals. However, the most important job of management accountant is t condoct a relevant cost analysis to determine the existing expenses and give suggestion for the future activities and make better management accounting, when management accountants need to learn how to apply these management accounting data: financial planning, financial statement analysis, cost accounting, find flow and cash flow analysis, standard , marginal cost and budgetary control, they can be made by AI.

In general, the job dutures of management accountant may include: generate sale among client accounts, operates as the point of contact for assigned customers, develops and maintains long term relationships with accounts, makes sure clients receives requested produsts ans services in a timely fashion . So, they need to learn these different management accounting technique: margin analys, capital budget, inventory valuation and product cost, tend analysis and forecasting. Future AI may be taught to learn all of these any one management accounting technique to assist organizations to make more reasonable management account strategy implementation.

The basic principles of management accounting include communication presents insight which is crucial , irrelevance information is valuable, the influence one value is estimated, credibility,recognizing the requirement, good accounting manager, they need to learn how conflict, be open to new ideas: In management accounting tehnology apply, there are three elements of management control system to develop to future Artificial intelligent management accounting technology delegated decison authority , performance evaluation and measurement systems and compensation, reward system.

Hence, accounting technology in AI development has always played a past in making the accountant's job just a played a part in making the accountant's job just a easier. Its own knowledge of technology increased to have the accountant's ability to analyze statistical values. Technology advancements have enhanced the accountant's ability to interpret data efficiently and effectively.

● Future AI management accountant may help human to the honest accounting record

However, any one managment accountant needs have good professional personal quality, honestly and integrity play vital roles in accounting because they allow investors to trust the information they receive about companies in which they invest. Honesty in accounting is the primary characteristics of the profession that allows financial decision-makers to make appropriate judgement . So, the main focus of management accounting is to assist the management of a company in efficiency performing its function-planning, organizaing, divesting and controlling . Management accounting helps with these functions in the following ways: provides data, it serves to a vital source of data for planning, for product costing method example, it is used to cost methods available are process costing, job and different production and decision making. for 3 types of controls may include: internal controls are typically procedures or technical safe guards that are implemented to prevent problems and protect organizations' assets. Future AI technology may help an organizations to do above all management accounting decision jobs ,even replace human in offices to avoid losses. The traditional management accounting technique includes" the use of performance measures, three ROI , budget systems for planning and control, divisional profit reports and cost-profit volume relationship, and breakeven analysis for decisions. The management accounting reports may include order information report, project report, competitor analysis. They are either internally aor outsourced. All of these management accounting methods, future AI can replace human accountants to do .

- Can AI be applied to help organizations to implement management account strategies ?

The two widely used types of accounting are: Financial and management accoutning, for the strategic cost management techniques example, it is the cost management techniques that aims at reducing cost , when strengthening the position of the business. It is a process of combining the decision making structure with the cost information in order to do the strategy as a whole . Hence the role of management account in the organization is to support competitive decision making by collecting, processing and communicating information that helps management plan, control and evaluating business processes and company strategy . So, the strategy management accounting can be defined as the process of identifying, collecting , selecting and analyzing accounting data . So, future AI can be applied to assist accounting teams in strategic decision making and organization effectiveness assessment must be defined.

Future AI can be applied to these management accounting aspect: For methods and techniques of costing management , it may include: Job costing, advestment, salepeople,bonus, contract cost, long periods of time job, batch cost, process cost, one operation ( unit or output) , cost service or operating costing, farm cost, multiple cooperation unit. The tools of cost analysis, breakeven analysis, budget cost control marginal cost analysis, cost control , minimum price analysis, standard cost development , target cost. All of these management strategies, AI can do .

The various tools and technique of marginal costing may include: contribution, profit volume ratio, contribution : sale value , p/v ratio, features of profit volume , break even point . Hence, the AI tools can control cost monitoring in execution. For that AI can help organizations to make cost control budget, it is defined as a AI tool that is used by the management of an organization in regulating and controlling of a manufacturing organization. AI can also perform cost budget for material to any manufacturing organizations to help them to reduce the manufacturing cost , e.g. making material choice for the cheapest price.

AI can gather the product material price, e.g. standard cost and normal cost. Then , AI can help the manufacturing organization to choose thc best quality of the cheapest material in order to compare whether which kinds of material to produce the kind of product can bring the high economic benefit to let consumers get more satisfactory feeling. Thus, it is future management accounting development direction for AI.

Ecommerce organization resource management strategy

Why does in this e-commerce organization situation, online webstore speed must be the most important factor to influence its sale success. Information technology internet speed, online webstore design, online transation convenience transaction feeling ( tangibale and intangible both resource factors ) may influence its future clients number ?

In behavioral economic view, any organizations must need to use resources to carry on any business or working activities. Resources may include: management time to managements, working time to employees, information technology etc. office computer to administration, factory equipment to plant workers, plant or warehouse land space to logistic delivery or goods shelves, electricity, gas , water to workplace , even, employees number. HR to any department tasks. So, it seems that before any organization can finish any activities, they must need enough resources supply in order to satisfy any activities need. If the organization overall itself , even overall society. I shall explain as below:

For ecommerce organizatin example, any online trading firms must need to own high speed internet information technology resource to supply to any one technologic staff store to pay visa to buy any product in the most short time rapidly. So, its online store website speeds must need to be very fast in order to avoid to delay any country clients to carry on online transaction. If the ecommerce business organization can not support efficient, high speed internet service to let any countries online buyers to satisfy its online webstore purchase service. Then, any countries‘ online buyers may choose another online store to replace to buy its similar product easily.

Hence, convenient webstore online purchase service much be very important to influence this online webstore organization. It seems that technologic online internet resource must be the most influential factor to influence this online websore organization clients number. If its online website store can not supply rapid online purchase speed to let any one country to buy its products from its webstores rapidly. Then, its clients number may be influenced to reduce. So, in this e-commerce organization situation, online webstore speed must be the most important factor to influence its sale success. Information technology internet speed, online webstore design, online transation convenience transaction feeling ( tangibale and intangible both resource factors ) may influence its future clients number . So, judging whether the kind of resource is the most important to influence the organization's success, it depends on whether it needs to use what kind of resource to carry on its daily activities.

In fact, one organizational change has relationship to whether its reponses can have enough supply as well as its behavior can be influenced by the resources variable , the scarcity of any kinds of resources are supplied to be used. So, I believe that whether any kinds of resources are scarcity in the organizational environment, how much they are used, these any kind of resources can bring relationship to influence how organizational perceptions, interpretations and responses.

How an ecommerce organization resource affects society?

Why has online webstore's information technology resource close relationship t influence online buyers number and social job chance?

Organizational impact to the effect on an organization has any reponses to influence how on society chance. However, organizations can also have a positive impact on the economic satisfaction of a town. More oe less jobs supply to the wociety, which can be influenced by whether the organization can have effort to buy how much resources to be used in order to carry on itself any business activities. Hence, it seems that if the organization, such as the above online website sale product organization, if it can have enough money to employ web design professional to help it to design attractive website stores to let attract online buyer purchase choice, as well as paid higher internet service fee to improve its fee to improve its online internet speed in order to let any countries online customers can still click its website rapidly, even in busy online click time. Many people click computer mouse to enter ecommerce website stores in the same time. Then, any one won't choose another websites stores to replace its online sale service easily. Even, if it can buy many advanced computers to let its staffs can use the best quality computers to follow any client's ourchase transaction in short time. When , they confirm that whether the client's visa card payment can accept and what product he has paid to buy from its webstore. Then, the staff can know where the accurate address of the country , the client's product can be delivered rapidly. It will avoid to delay any product delivery. So, if this online store seller can have enough internet information technology source to support its whole computer information department staffs to wrk efficiently. Then, it can increase more online transaction chance in success. Consequently, it can grow up its online sale business, it will create many new potisition, due to its computer information technology department must need to increase employees to help it to deal any countries online buyers online purchase service transactions and online product sale delivery service immediately in order to avoid online product delivery service to global online buyers. So, it can bring more job chance if this online webstore organization can have enough effort to buy high technological computer information products to let its online customer service staffs to use in order to improve online product delivery service store to let global many online buyers' attention . Consequently, it can apply online webstore purchase channel to apply website purchase channel to persuade many global online buyers online purchase choice to its webstore easily. So, it seems that this online webstore's information technology resource has close relationship t influence online buyers number and social job chance.

How do organizational resources affect organizational change?

IN general, resoults indicate that organizations possessing greater stocks of historically valuable resources were much less likely to engage in adaptive strategic change, but also that this resource-driven disinclination towards change tended to have a begin or even beneficial effect on performance . So, in general, if one organization lacks any one of these three important resources. It can influence this organization's performance to worse, they many include: human resource , financial resource, phycial resources and information resource. However, managers are responsible to acquiring and managing the resources to accomplish goals. If the organization can have enough resources to be used. It can bring positive impact to influence its overall organizational performance, even, when it has not any resource scarcity, it can avoid negative impacts on the society, such as increasing jobs chance. Hence, scarcity of capital, human and social resources to be provided to the organization, it will influence the organizational structure changes, even employee individual work attitude is influenced to change worse, when he/she can not have the best resources to be used in order to raise efficiency or improve performance more easily.

How to build organizatonal resource using right psychology

The psychology of management is the branch of psychology studying mental features of the person and its behavior in the course of planning, organization management and the control of joint activity. The human factor is considered as the central point in the psychology of management as its essence and a core. Hence , organizational psychology plays a very important rolw at the time or recruitment very important role at the time of recruitment taking disciplinary action or resolving disputes between employees. HR focus and expertise mainly lies in dealing with people . So , it makes sense that the study of the human mind, how to use organizational resources efficiently.

The organizational side of pschology is more focused on understanding how organizations affect individual behavior, organizational structures , social norms, management styles and role expectations are factors that can influence how people behave within organizations. In general, industrial organizational psychologists use psychological principles and research methods to solve problems in the workplace and improve the quality of life ( e.g. avoiding often waste industrial resources in manufacturing process aims). They study workplace workplace productivity and management and employee working styles. They get a feel for the morale and personality of a company or organization, e.g. suggesting to use skills and knowledge relating to psychology how to reduce same productivity level, but the organizational resources can be reduced to use. It is one kind the most efficiency resources using method to any kind of organizations.

On conclusion, industrial and organizational psychologists will often use science to study human behavior organizations and the workplaces. Their aims to help organizations to reduce excess resource using in any manufacturing process in order to reduce cost. Employers who need to attempt to learn how employees use resources to do work activities, it can bring these advanaages : learning how to use neuroscience to attract the right talent, retain high performing employees, because any organizations‘ resources will be used in order to manufacture any products or work activites by any employees in any time.

Employees are the ones who get the job done. They know how the organization and especially ho w their specigif team works best. So any one employee may be the important factor to influence the amount of resource use, any organizational resource use amount, it has close relationship to any employee work behavior. Moreover, resources, that is , group-level resources associated with shared relationship that foster a quality exchange of information and interaction between individuals within the workplace , helping any one employee to learn more about on the job training, use employee training optios to ensure department leader optimizes the employees' motiviation and potential retention. Aim to give opinions to employees to know how to avoid resource using waste method to achieve cost saving aim to the organization.

CHAPTER SIX

# LEARNING HOW RESOURCES CHANGE SOCIAL BEHAVIOR

Human Behavioral network job brings social economic benefits

What does human network job mean ? Why may human network job be popular? Why human network job behavior may influence economy ?

Nowadays internet is popular to use. We can apply internet to find data , search any new things, even earn money. Why does internet may become huma network job source. For example, e-publish may be one kind of new human network job. Any authors may apply internet

channel to help them to sell electronic or paper books from e-publisher web store. They may apply facebook, you tub etc. any online

channel to promote themselves new books to let new readers to know whether when they may buy themselves favourable new topic books to read

from electronic publisher web store.

Thus, future electronic publisher industry may help any authors to build internet network platform to help them to sell and promote ot advertise their any one new electronic or paper book topic to let global any one reader to choose to buy their any new topic books from electronic publisher web store easily and conveniently. However, it implies that electronic network platform author may be one kind of future new human network job in our societies.

How electronic network platform author job may bring economy benefit in macro economy view? A person can have few friends, contacts and still be very influential if these few
friends and contacts are themselves highly influential, e.g. one author must not need to know any one reader in global society. When they like to choose any electronic books from electronic internet network platform. They may become the author's any one topic book buyer, when they feel the author's any one topic book is fun and attract they make decision to buth the strange author whose the topic book from electronic book publisher's platform web store conventiently in short time. Although, they are strangers, they do not know themselves , but the reader can understand what it way that made Google from writing platofrm to create new creative mind and typing network job method to replace traditional hand writing book method for global authors. It will be one kind of new human network writing job.

Hence, global any one reader can apply an innovative search engine , such as google.com to find whether whom author personal new topic books are value to read from internet.
Then, the electroniuc publisher's web store may be new book store platform sale network to help the author to sell many electronic or paper books from electronic network platform
in short time. So, internct may be future new network plaform to help global any one author to create network writing job absolutely. Furthermore, internet may be popular social media
to help any one author to build goold relationship between his/her readers. It is one kind of new network, human network job. New authors do not need to buy many paper books to prepare to put in any one book shop warehouse. Their every book can print on demand to reduce out of book stock in any one book shop.

They may choose to sell either electronic books or paper books both from any one book publisher web store. So, electronic network platform may be one kind of good writing channel to help human authors to create income and it can also
help authors to bring new creative mind and new topic fun content books to let readers to know and buy to read from electronic publisher network platform.

Why does human behavior may be one kind of new human network job to bring global economic advantages. ALthough, it may be free income or without inocme, but the person does the network behavior, his/her behavior may be bring advantages to influence many other people's health. For this case, when a worker in a coffee shop in an airport gets a vaccination aganinst the flu, it does not only helps him or her stay healthy, but also helps the many travellers who might otherwise have been inflected if that workers caught the flu.
So, the externality , the result implies the vaccination of even a part of a community conveys benefits to the whole community. For example, governments pay special attention
to the vaccinations of school children, teachers, health mothers, and the elderly, categories of people particularly susceptible not only to catching, but also to transmitting a disease.

It is not accidential that governments are heavily involved with vaccination . When there are externalities, free market, fail to persuade individual incentives with society's
their the worker's decision of whether to get a vaccine ends up attracting whether other people get sick. The workers might not fully take all these other people's potential suffering into account when making her or his vaccination decision.

As Stanford University does many suggestions, understand this and tries to help them make the right decisions and so providers free flu vaccines for its staff and students.
Small pockets of unvaccinated individuals can allow a disease to gain a spread more widely well-being. For example, parent weighing the costs and benefits of a vaccine for their child is not always

thinking of the consequences of that vaccination to other people. THese are markets in which subsidizing or regulating behavior can make everyone better off. Because the reason for requiring that a child be vaccinated before enrolling in school is not just to protect that child, because each child's vaccination affects others via potential contagions.

Robots take our jobs behavioral and economy influences

Robot job behavior brings economy influences

If one day robots can replace human to do simple, even complex jobs. They will bring what influences to our global societial economy.The popular economic refrain declares that the global middle class is dying and robots will soon take our jobs, e.g. shopping center customer service jobs, library service jobs, cinema ticket sale jobs, restaurant kitchen cooker jobs, even, bus drivers, taxi drivers etc. public transport driving jobs, accountant, doctors etc. professional jobs. Whether it is beautiful or petty matter if our future societies have many human jobs can be replaced to do from robots. Businessman must may reduce to employ employees and reduce to pay salary or wage, when robots can be replaced to do their employees tasks. But, societies must bring unemployement rate rises , due to societies will have many people loss jobs when their employers choose to buy robots to serve their clients or do any office tasks or customer service or cleaning etc. tasks.

In micro economy view, employers may save money in long term, but in macro economy view, it will cause unemployment ratio rises , even crime rate rises when there are many people lose jobs in societies. These models of doom, though, fail to account for the hundreds of businesses riding the waves of change in their industries when robots may be invented to replace human to do many simple , even complex tasks in our future societies.

WE may image that one small factory needs to manufacture fishes canes to sell to supermarket, the small , cheaper stuff and

higher margin parts of the fishes manufacture industry. Before, this factory needs to employe many human factory workers need to help every fresh customer makeing the perfect fishing gear, designed for performance, durability, and cost in order to achieve to manufacture every fish cane in whole fished processing manufacturing stages. Every worker needs to spend about 15 to twenty minutes to finish every fish cane , till to delivery to any supermarket to sell. If this fish canes manufacturing factory can apply manufacturing robots to help them to finish any one working tasks , every robot can only spend five minutes to finish whole fresh fish cane manufacturing process. Thus, every robot can help this factory save 10 to 15 minutes time to finsh every fish cane manufacturing process. IN fact, time is money, because when every robot can help this factory to reduce 10 to 15 minutes time to compare human worker. Then, this factory can finish about 20 fish canes in one hour if it can use robot to help it to manufacture fish canes. Otherwise, if this factory still use human workers to help it to manufacture fish canes, then it can finsh about 3 to 4 fish canes in one hour. SO, the manufacturing efficiency ensures that robots must help this fish manufacturing factory to raise fish canes number more than human workers. So, in robotic behavioral economy view, manufacturing robots must help this fish canes manufacturing factory to raise fish canes manufacturing number and deliver increasing number to supermarkets to prepare to sell every day. Robots can help this fish canes manufacturing factory bring manufacturing time saving, rising manufacturing efficiency, improving performance and reducing wages expenditure long time advantages in micro economy view. However, manufacturing robots can also bring disadvanages to society, e.g. increasing unemployment ratio, increasing crime rate,
this factory workers will lose jobs and income, they need earn social welfare from government and increasing government finance pressure in short time, even long time in macro economic view.

Stanford University graduate program in economics, Scott lecturer explained that "in demand and supply economic theory for robots supply and demand case, robots supply number increasing may influence human workers demand number decrease. It sometimes calls " the efficient frontier".

No specific human beings were mentioned in any of economics classes. As robots supply and demand in market case, They ( robots) may be purely theoretical " agents" who reached to the most reasonable sale prices in order to persuade any one businessman buyer to make manufacturing robot buying decision whether robots can help him / her to bring how much saving time , saving money, saving cost, improving performance, efficiency economic benefit before he/she plans to reduce workers number when he/she decides to apply robots to replace human workers in his/her factory or office or any service department, e.g. cinema ticket sale service, shopping center customer service, shopping center cleaning , supermarket customer service etc. service or sale tasks. When robots can replace human to do any one of these tasks in any organizations. So, robots may be human worker agents who reached to prices the way robots would react to a software
command. There was nothing that explained why some people thrived and others did n't or why truly brilliant, hardworking people could fail when much lazier folks succeeded." Having been admitted to the Stanford University graduate program in economics, Scott lecturer hoped to get his answers there.

How robots influence our future social changing? Using the right technology can be a boon to your business in this economy. For internet example, it is easier than ever to find well-matched customers
all around the world, to stay in contact with them, and to more quickly design the products they want. If you focus solely on being cutting -edge, though you risk letting the technology
take over what should be very robust relationships with your customers , employees, and colleagues. IN nowaddays society, technoligical advances and cutomation, personal
relationships in business are more crucial than ever. I mean that robots can not replace human to serve clients to let them to feel

more comfortable and passion more easily. For shoe shop case example, if the shoe shop apply one robot to serve its clients to replace human shoe salesperson to serve its shoe customers. Robots ensure that they can not persuade every shoe potential buyer to make shoe buying decision more easily when robots need to contact every shoe potential buyer. The reason is simple, because robots can not touch any one shoe buyer individual emotion very easier.

If the shoe buyer needs the robots to help him/her to choose any right shoe styles when he/she can not feel himself / herself can make the most right shoe style choice decision. The robots can not replace human shoe salesperson to make shoe style choice judgement more easily. They must need longer time to analyze whether which shoe style may be the most suitable to the shoe buyer. Otherwise,human shoe salesperson may attempt to make the most right shoe style choice decision to help any one shoe buyer to chooce the most right style shoe because he/she owns shoe style sale experience, shoe style knowledge, the most important reason is that they can feel every shoe customer individual emotion to touch whether he/she will feel comfortable or happy when they attempt to help every shoe customer to seek the most right shoe style in every shoe customer whole shoe searching processing. Othwerwise, serving robots are only one machine, they can not touch or feel every shoe customer individual emotion whether he/she feel comfortable or unhappy or happy when they need to contact them in whole shoe searching processing. Hence, I believe that some tasks robots can not repalce human staff to do very easily. Otherwise, robots may bring disadvanatges to let any one businessman to loss his/her customers, due to robots can not touch every customer

emotion to compare human staff in service tasks more easily. Robots serving customer behaviors may cause money lose and customers number lose to the shop in micro economic view.

Intellectual human economic behaviors

What does intellectual human economic behaviors mean ? I believe that when we choose or decide to do intellectual behaviors, then our societies will be influenced to bring economic growth in consequence.I shall attempt to indicate pollution case to explain how and why eithet our intellectual or foolish behaviors may bring economic growth or recession in consequence as below:

On one hand, for air pollution social case aspect example, if we only consider to buy cars to drive for working aimr or holiday leisure aim. Then, our societies air will be polluted. Our health will be influenced to bad. Our car driving behaviors may cause global environment air pollution serously. In long tiem, global air pollution will bring our bodies health to be bad. Although, ourselves car driving behaviors may bring our driving travelling leisure enjoyment and comfortable feeling in short time, also we so not need to pay public transport fare often, but we need to compensate ourselves health economic intangible loss due to air pollution , when cars number increases, dirty air will cause ouselves health to become bad.

In the result, we will need to pay more medical expenditure when we are old age, due to ourselves bodies will become bad, due to we breathe global dirty air every day, due to ourselves cars pollute air in long time, e.g. 10 to 20 years, even 30 more without limited air pollution environment. So, driving cars behavior may be one kind of human foolish behavior and our foolish behavior may bring ourselves future long time medical expenditure absolutely.

One the other hand, water pollution social aspect, if we often keep much rubblish to pollute sea, oil exploration porcessing pollute ocean , ships gas pollute ocaen, then fishes will eat polluted food and drive dirty water, due to global ocean is polluted.

In fact, because human only to conside how to buy boats to carry on leisure enjoyment activities, or catch cruises to travel on the sea. Also, oil manufacturers only consider researching anywhere to find new oil exploration places to manufacture oil product, when their oil exploration processes pollute ocarn . Consequently, global fishes drink polluted warer or eat polluted food. They will have poison. SO, human will have high chance to eat poison polluted fishes, due to fishes are poison or are polluted.

So, human is doing foolish activities, we only hope to find oil exploration places to pollute ocean or we only spend money to buy ticket to catch ships to travel anywhere in global ocean. All of these human foolish behaviors will bring pollution to global ocean. On consequently, we will need to compensate to eat polluted or dirty or poision fishes, ourselves bodies health will be bad. In long time, we need have high chance to pay medical expenditure when we are old. So, pollution case may be one good example to explain how and why human foolish behavior may influence ourselves future need to compensate serious medical loss.

All of these human foolish behavior will bring pollution to global ocean. On consequently, we will need to compensate to eat polluted or dirty or poison fished , ourselves bodies health will be bad. In long time, we will have high chance to pay medical expenditure, when we are old. So, pollution case may be one good example to explain how and why human ourselves intellectual or foolish behaviors may influence future long time economic loss or economic growth or recession in micro and micro economic view.

On another water pollution aspect hand, if we often keep rubbish to sea, oil exploration processing pollutes ocean and ships' gas pollute ocean, then fishes will eat polluted food and drink dirty water, due to fishes will eat polluted food and drink dirty sea water because the global ocean is polluted seriously.

In fact, because human only consider how to buy boats to carry on any leisure water activities, or catches cruises to travel on the sea. Also, oil manufacturers only consider any where to find oil exploratin places to manufacture oil products from ocean, when their pol exploration processes can plooute ocean. Consequently, global fishes drink polluted water or eat direty food. They will have poison. So, human will have high chance to eat poison fishes.

Otherwise, such as pollution case, it can infuence inflation or deflation. Consequently, the reason indicates supply and demand theory. If air pollution is serious, then we will consider health issue, global cars demand number may be influenced to reduce, when global cars number demand will reduce, global car prices and supply number will need to change to fall down in order to attract or persuade global car consumers choose to make car purchase decision.

Hence, global car manufacture number and car price will be influenced to reduce, due to global air pollution issue. Consequently, deflation will occur because when the country citizen usually does not spend much extra saving money to buy car expensive goods. Money value will be low. Otherwise, if global cair pollution is not serious, human considers to buy cars to enjoy driving leisure lives. So, global car demand is influenced to increase , also global car price will also influenced to increase.

Consequently, gobal human will choose to buy cars to drive. Due to we accept to spend extra saving to buy expensive car goods. Car sale price and supply may be influenced to rise up. Money value is influenced to reduce. Inflation may be influenced, due to global car consumers number increases, we would not have extra money to spend easily. Car expensive goods expenditure influences our spending habit to avoid to make car purchase decision more easily. So, human intellectual or foolish activities may bring inflation or deflation consequency in possible indirectly in macro economic view.

On conclusion, above pollution case explain that how and why human intellectual or foolish economic behaviors may bring inflation or deflation consequency as wll as economic growth or recession consequency as well as any goods demand and supply increasing or decreasing consequency. It implies that human behavior may have indirect relationship to influence any goods demand and supply number to either increase or decrease result as well as any goods price will be influenced to increase or decrease in micro and macro economic view.

9 798887 726908

Printed by Libri Plureos GmbH in Hamburg,
Germany